#ReHumanize

meaningful relationships . . . but that's exactly what you get. I'm convinced that this book will not only make you more effective in business, but it will open your eyes to a more authentic approach to living life."

—*James Carbary, founder of Sweet Fish Media and cohost of*
The B2B Growth Podcast

rehumanize
YOUR BUSINESS

How **Personal Videos** Accelerate Sales
and Improve Customer Experience

ETHAN BEUTE + STEPHEN PACINELLI

WILEY

Published by John Wiley & Sons, Inc., Hoboken, New Jersey.
Published simultaneously in Canada.

For general information on our other products and services or for technical support, please contact our Customer Care Department within the United States at (800) 762-2974, outside the United States at (317) 572-3993 or fax (317) 572-4002.

Wiley publishes in a variety of print and electronic formats and by print-on-demand. Some material included with standard print versions of this book may not be included in e-books or in print-on-demand. If this book refers to media such as a CD or DVD that is not included in the version you purchased, you may download this material at http://booksupport.wiley.com. For more information about Wiley products, visit www.wiley.com.

Library of Congress Cataloging-in-Publication Data:

Names: Beute, Ethan, 1973- author. | Pacinelli, Stephen, 1977- author.
Title: Rehumanize your business : how personal videos accelerate sales and
   improve customer experience / Ethan Beute, Stephen Pacinelli.
Description: Hoboken, New Jersey : John Wiley & Sons, Inc., [2019] | Includes
   index. |
Identifiers: LCCN 2018060340 (print) | LCCN 2019001723 (ebook) | ISBN
   9781119576280 (ePub) | ISBN 9781119576273 (ePDF) | ISBN 9781119576266
   (hardcover)
Subjects: LCSH: Internet marketing. | Internet videos. | Customer relations.
Classification: LCC HF5415.1265 (ebook) | LCC HF5415.1265 .B487 2019 (print)
   | DDC 658.8/72—dc23
LC record available at https://lccn.loc.gov/2018060340

Cover Design: Ava Gretzinger and Leah Von Fange

Printed in the United States of America

V10008520 030519

DEDICATION

To our families, to our team members,
and to everyone who values relationships
over transactions.

CONTENTS

ACKNOWLEDGMENTS

One of the themes throughout this book is that our personal and professional successes result not just from our own efforts but through others' efforts, too. Our true wins come with, through, and for other people. We'd like to acknowledge Conor McCluskey, Darin Dawson, and the entire BombBomb team—every person in every seat in every department. This book would not be possible without you. We thank all of the personal video pioneers who allowed us to share their stories in this book and all of you whose stories we'll have to tell in blog posts, on webinars, and from stages. Thanks to every one of our customers and our critics; you inspire us to work harder and be better every day. And thanks to Richard Narramore at Wiley to whom the concept felt a little early but still had the vision to bring this to market.

FROM STEVE: Thank you, Gretchen. You made me the person I am today through the kindest heart I've ever known. Thank you, Grant and Owen, for showing me what it's like to overcome any obstacle. Sophia, thank you, for completing our little, big family and for bringing so much joy and laughter. Dad, Mom, Jennifer, Aimee, and the rest of my family and friends, thank you for providing all the love, warmth, and support a person could need. And finally, Ethan, you are a true role model in business and in life. I strive to be more like you. Thank you.

FROM ETHAN: Thank you, Megan and Owen, for your constant encouragement, patience, support, and inspiration through every endeavor. Thanks to Steve for adding so much value and fun to this project, my work, and my life. Thanks to Chris Smith, Thor Iverson, Dan Steinman, and Kurt Bartolich for sharing insights into your writing and publishing processes. Thanks to all the great teachers, leaders, and mentors who've broadened my perspective and provided challenge. Love to my mom, whom we lost this year, and to my family, who learned so much from her about relationships and connection.

ABOUT THE AUTHORS

ETHAN BEUTE

Ethan has collected and told personal video success stories in hundreds of blog posts, in dozens of webinars, podcasts, and stage presentations, and in countless conversations. He spent a dozen years leading marketing teams inside local television stations in Chicago, Grand Rapids, and Colorado Springs. His undergraduate and graduate degrees from the University of Michigan and UCCS in communication, psychology, and marketing were conferred with highest distinction. Ethan is Vice President of Marketing at BombBomb, and currently resides in Colorado Springs with his wife and son.

STEPHEN PACINELLI

Before becoming CMO at BombBomb, Steve was a customer and advocate of personal video for its benefits to his sales team. As a Sales Manager, Vice President of Events, and National Speaker for Realtor.com, Steve was a featured speaker who's delivered presentations to more than 1,000 audiences. A passionate storyteller by nature and the most extroverted introvert you'll ever meet, Steve resides in Downingtown, Pennsylvania, with his wife, twin boys, and daughter.

Introduction

Do you ever misread emails or text messages? Or have your emails or text messages ever been misunderstood?

Are you tired of cold calling and sending cold emails? Or of feeling like you're interrupting or bothering people?

Have you ever felt embarrassed by your spelling, grammar, or punctuation? Or has autocorrection ever caused you trouble?

Yes. Yep. Affirmative.

Would you save time by doing more talking and less writing?

If you got face to face with more people, would you create and close more opportunities?

Yup. Absolutely.

And yet every day you continue to entrust some of your most important and therefore most valuable messages to faceless digital communication. The same black text on the same white screen that doesn't build trust, doesn't differentiate you, and doesn't communicate as well as if you just looked someone in the eye and said the exact same message.

The pendulum's swung too far away from the personal touch and human connection that drive your success and satisfaction. It's time to rehumanize your business. No matter the product, service, company, brand, or idea you represent, when people say "yes," they're saying yes to *you*. To who you are. With the strategies and tactics you'll learn in this book, you can get to "yes" faster by being more personal and human.

What does it mean to rehumanize your business? It means being more, well, human. Restoring a face-to-face element that's gone missing. Being more intentional and personal in your approach. Building better business relationships. Recognizing that you're truly winning when you win with, through, and for other people. Treating people the way you prefer to be treated. "Targeting" and "hunting" less and connecting and serving more.

What's one of the best ways to do this? By adding personal videos to your emails, text messages, and social messaging. Not videos for marketing, but rather videos for relationships. Not videos that are scripted, produced, and edited, but rather videos that are conversational, authentic, and imperfect. Videos that save time, improve results, and increase satisfaction—your own and that of your customers, future customers, and everyone else with a stake in your success. This is your new *and* old way to sell and serve—using today's technology to make sales and service truly personal again.

Building trust, rapport, and relationships are best done in person, but time and distance have increasingly driven us to faceless, digital messages. To make matters worse, most of us aren't very good writers; our messages are often misunderstood or require longer exchanges to arrive at mutual understanding. Video puts *you* back into your communication in a way that accelerates sales and improves customer experience. It restores that missing face-to-face element. But now you can get face to face *at scale*. All through quick, simple video messages with the webcam or smartphone camera you've always got with you.

Get face to face *at scale* with simple, personal videos.

If you're in leadership or management, inside or outside sales, account-based marketing, recruiting or talent development, or customer support or success, you'll be more successful when you rehumanize your processes by mixing in video messages. If you're in software, consulting, education, real estate, mortgage, insurance, financial planning, automotive, nonprofit, public speaking, entrepreneurship, or almost any other role or industry, this applies to you. Anyone working in a professional capacity benefits from better relationships. And video does this better than any other medium except being there in person.

Because you're reading this intro, you may already be sending video or at least you may have given it a look or tried it out. With more than a decade of experience and unique expertise, Steve and I offer practical and proven strategies, tips, and insights to help you implement video day to day. If you've not given it a look or tried it out, you likely know someone who is "doing video." Have you ever heard someone say that?

"I don't do video. But Mary does video."

"Yeah, Mary does do video. I tried video. Do you do video?"

"No, I don't do video, either."

Replace "video" with "phone calls" or "email" or "meetings." For example . . .

"I don't do phone calls. But Mary does phone calls."

"Yeah, Mary does do phone calls. I tried phone calls. Do you do phone calls?"

"No, I don't do phone calls, either."

Sounds silly, right? Well, that's where we're headed. Because "doing video" no longer requires scripts, lights, editing, or budgets. "Doing video" means occasionally recording a webcam or smartphone video in place of a typed-out message, a phone call, or even a meeting. In the pages ahead, you're going to learn why, how, and when to make video part of your business communication mix.

My coauthor Steve got going with this video philosophy as he searched for a better way to sell software. He deployed personal video email to the members of his outside sales team as a way to generate more revenue both on and off the road. With video in place of text, they built value before getting to price, shortened the sales cycle, and closed multiple $24,000 annual contracts with people they'd never met in person and never even talked with over the phone. He transitioned from a BombBomb video email user to our Chief Marketing Officer a few years later and more than four years ago.

My engagement started with part-time projects—creating a homepage video, writing an email nurture campaign, recording videos for those emails, and other deliverables for a couple of friends, Conor McCluskey and Darin Dawson. After founding the company a few years earlier, they were preparing to bring to market a video email service. Bored after more than a decade of traditional and digital marketing for local television stations, I was doing project work on the side with several other companies, too. But I exclusively locked onto this idea and locked in with this team for its forward-looking nature and rehumanizing potential.

Most new technology is understood in terms of its predecessor and video email is no exception. I viewed our initial product offering as an email marketing platform with video uploading and hosting built right in. And, as a product, that's what it was at the time—and I fully expected MailChimp or even Google to devour the available market for it by rolling out a similar feature set. Through constant and direct customer contact (something I rarely had in my broadcast television career), it became clear that we weren't just a "video email marketing" service. This mental shift or change in understanding is most clear in the increasing gap between "marketing through video" and "relationships through video."

In this book, you'll get language, understanding, and practical applications of this rapidly emerging trend of rehumanizing communication, accelerating sales, and improving customer experience with video. It's about realigning some of your day-to-day efforts with millennia of human brain training that dictates how we communicate and connect with each other. It's about evolving tactics and improving results. It's about how and why a salesperson sent his 12,000th video—and the likelihood he's the first person to create that volume of video to build relationships and increase sales. It's about being there in person when you *can't* be there in person.

Over the past decade, we've watched our own community grow from about 100 active, paying customers to well over 40,000. They live all around the world and work in all kinds of industries. We've learned and taught from their success stories and examples in hundreds of blog posts, webinars, podcasts, stage presentations, and, of course, videos. We've seen other companies come "down market" from prescribing scripted, lighted, produced, and edited videos to recommending our "video voicemail" style videos. We've read about multibillion-dollar companies like Coca-Cola and Levi Strauss & Co. intentionally reducing the quality of their photos and videos to make them appear more trustworthy to consumers, a phenomenon we'd described years earlier as the "Shiny/Authenticity Inversion." With a growing range of companies, communities, and individuals getting involved, this movement is just getting started.

> Now is the time to start using video for relationships, not just for marketing.

In Part One, you'll learn what personal video is, why it's rehumanizing compared to the status quo, and why you should participate. In Part Two, you'll see who's using personal video and when you might use it, too. Part Three is the how—recording and sending, cameras and equipment, psychological barriers, and more. Part Four delivers advanced strategies and a look to the future of this growing movement. Throughout, you'll get practical tips to replace some of your typed-out text with a more personal and human touch.

And, no, the irony is not lost on us that this is all being shared by way of simple black text on a plain white page.

PART 1

Why It's Time to
Rehumanize Your Business

CHAPTER 1

———

The New Way to Communicate, Connect, and Convert

We see each other once or twice a year, but my sister doesn't call often. My wife talks with her more often than I do. We keep up through social media, text messages, and a phone call every now and then. So, when she called on a weekday in the late afternoon, I knew I needed to answer.

"Hey, what's up?" I asked.

"Umm . . . Mom's dead," she quietly replied. Calm, but without confidence, she followed with an apology. "Sorry to be so blunt. I didn't know how else to say it."

Our mom died unexpectedly in early 2018. She felt dizzy, fell down, and never got back up. She was at home with my dad, sister, and nephew doing what she often did—rushing back into the kitchen to get that one final dish to complete a dinner already on the table. A two-time cancer survivor, she was in a great phase of her life after losing weight, replacing a knee, working out with a personal trainer, and traveling a lot more to see her kids, her grandkids, her friends, and the tropics. All that positive momentum made the phone call even harder to take than it would have been otherwise.

A few days later, I flew back to my hometown of Grand Rapids, Michigan. The first visitation was on a Friday evening. Prior to it, we put together a few photo boards from the hundreds, if not thousands, of prints she'd made over the years; framed and magnet-pinned photos of family and friends lined her walls and bookshelves. Seeing her face through the years and seeing her with so many other smiling, familiar faces was a pleasure. We saw many of them in person that night; the volume and warmth of support for her and for our family was wonderful.

The next morning, we hosted the second visitation, which was followed by the funeral service. You know how these social occasions go. You don't keep your gaze fixed when you're in a conversation. With no disrespect to the person with whom you're talking, you glance around the room. As I stood and spoke with a supportive family friend that morning, I saw a familiar face over her shoulder. But it was an unexpected face; it didn't make complete sense in the moment. It felt like seeing your dental hygienist at Costco—without the uniform and the context of the office, you don't recognize the person as quickly. After I wrapped up the conversation, I headed over to him.

This gentleman greeted me with a soft smile and warm hug, as did his wife. I'd never met either of them in person. I'd never spoken with them on the phone. Neither one of them knew or had ever met my mom. Neither of them knew a single one of my family members. They knew no one else at the visitation. And yet they drove two hours across the state to spend three or four minutes with me. The gesture was incredibly meaningful; I can still feel the moment when my mind put together what they'd done.

What inspired them to invest more than half a day to create that brief, in-person meeting? Relationship. Our relationship was built through simple video messages recorded and sent back and forth, off and on over a couple years' time. And it's a real relationship. I felt as though I knew him before I ever met him—and I know he'd say the same about me. When we later swapped video messages about their visiting with me that day, he speculated, "That never would have happened through regular email. It was the video portion of our emails that caused that to happen. And that just enriches life."

> Video builds psychological proximity between people, even in the absence of physical proximity.

I now call Andy Alger a longtime BombBomb customer-turned-friend. A real estate agent in Grand Blanc, Michigan, he generates nearly all of his business from his database of past clients. Staying in contact meaningfully with just a few hundred people creates repeat business and personal referrals. Relationships, then, are fundamental to his success. I suspect he's made gestures like the one I experienced many times before in other people's lives.

To stay in touch with the new ways people are using video, we regularly look at the top customers in our database in terms of videos recorded and sent per day. We often reach out to learn about their motivations, strategies, and outcomes; this book is, in large part, the result of these efforts. Andy showed up on my radar pretty quickly. He signed up nearly five years ago and, in that time, has sent 4,000 videos. Back in April 2014, I reached out to learn more about what he was doing and why he was doing it. At the time, he was closing in on his 500th video. By one-to-one video, of course, he told me: "Personal videos make what I do fun again. And my clients respond to it very well—and, really, that's why I do it. I started it because I thought it was a neat idea, but then I saw the reaction of my clients and it's great. They love it. I love it."

To stay connected with the people who matter most to his business, Andy used to block out time on his calendar to make phone calls. But he increasingly felt like he was intruding on their day and interrupting their lives. A phone call became an imposition on his clients' time with which he grew less and less comfortable. Recording and sending videos, however, could be done on his own time. And each person plays his video and experiences the message whenever it's most convenient. One person might open it and see

Andy immediately. Another might see it 10 minutes later, another two hours later, and another three days later—whenever it's convenient.

> The asynchronicity of recording and sending personal videos provides convenience for both the sender and the receiver.

Because they provided a more effective and more satisfying way to work, simple webcam videos replaced phone calls as Andy's preferred way to stay in touch. In the same amount of time he'd block out for calls, he could record and send a couple dozen truly personal messages. One video for each person, couple, or family. Like a voicemail, but with his face, voice, personality, sincerity, enthusiasm, and all the elements that can't be delivered through faceless, digital communication. He delivers himself, in person, at scale. And unlike voicemail, video email allows him to know exactly who's opening the email and playing the video—and exactly when.

This method is less demanding and more respectful of people's time. Andy treats people as he himself prefers to be treated, getting his message across more personally, more often. This is what it can look like to rehumanize your business.

A SIMPLE VIDEO MAKES A BIG DIFFERENCE

Andy sprinted out of the gates with 488 videos sent in under five months. Averaging more than 100 videos per month and more than three videos per day every day of the week, he'd obviously found a few very specific ways to use video and committed to them. At that rate, the videos are always personal, one-to-one sends. To learn best practices and to teach others, I've regularly reached out over the years to people like Andy to share their tips, insights, and successes with others. Here are two ways I could've reached out to him. Figure 1.1 shows a nice, traditional email and Figure 1.2 represents a more personal approach.

Option One: Plain, Typed-Out Text

FIGURE 1.1 Traditional Email

New Message

Ethan Beute <ethan@bombbomb.com>

Big milestone and small favor, Andy

Hello, Andy!
First and foremost, thanks for being a BombBomb customer. We sincerely appreciate you making us part of how you connect and communicate with people.

My name is Ethan. I'm on the marketing team at BombBomb and I've got some exciting news for you: you're closing in on a big milestone - your 500th video recorded and sent. That's a great achievement! Especially since you've only been at it for 5 months.

Because a lot of people never get that far, would you please take a few minutes to reply to any or all of these questions? I'd love to write your answers up in a blog post to help them out.

- Why have you made such a commitment to video email in your business?
- Think back six months or a year. What were you doing then that you now do with simple, personal videos?
- What are some of your favorite ways to use video?
- Do you have a specific success story or winning outcome that you attribute to a video you sent?
- What's your top tip for someone just getting started with video?

Thanks so much for sharing your time and insights. And thanks again for making BombBomb even some small part of your business.

Continued success to you! Ethan.

Send

Option Two: Personal Video Email

FIGURE 1.2 Video Email

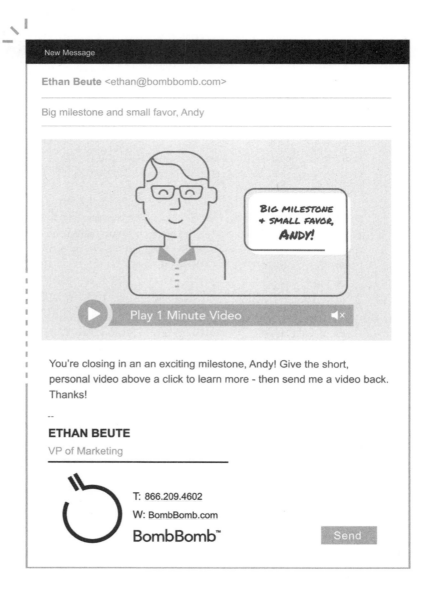

The Difference

Instead of constructing the 200-word email in Figure 1.1, I simply clicked "Record" and talked to Andy as if we were casually meeting in person. Instead of spending three or four minutes organizing my ideas into a well-structured email that didn't come across as pushy or demanding and didn't contain typos, misspellings, improper grammar, or egregious punctuation, I spent about 90 seconds speaking to him from my office through my webcam. Instead of relying on ALL CAPS, exclamation points, or emoticons to convey my excitement, I used an honest smile and my sincere enthusiasm to let him know how much I appreciated him and the milestone he was approaching. Instead of sending a laundry list of questions to answer, I asked the questions conversationally, just like I would in person. He then "knew" a person at our company. My smile and enthusiasm far outweighed any minor errors I may have made in the video—like an "um," a pause, or a misspoken word.

These are just a few reasons I went with the second option in Figure 1.2—and reasons why some of the messages you'll send this week shouldn't have two options anymore. With that video email, I improved communication, connection, and conversion with Andy, who complied, replied, and gave me more than I needed to publish a blog post. It was built from the excellent tips and insights he provided in his video reply. And I then "knew" one of our customers.

I shared this example because it's so specific to the story on which this chapter opened. The ideas and execution, though, can be used in situations you face every day at your desk, across town, or around the world. With recruits and employees, customers and future customers, partners and suppliers, or anyone else connected to your business. Just as there's an art and science to writing effective emails, there's an art and science to personal videos. Your success depends in part on whether or not you take advantage of concepts like:

- Introducing yourself for the first time through video instead of text
- Making clear in the email body that the video's personal, not automated
- Holding a whiteboard, sticky note, tablet, or another surface in your video thumbnail or animated preview with a custom note
- Writing on that surface her or his name, a relevant detail, a common interest, or another idea inspired by briefly researching the person (even draw a logo or picture)
- Adding a little text along with your video that encourages people to click to play

- Providing a simple reason ("because") along with your request or call to action
- Watching for notifications and alerts to confirm the email open and video play

Several elements are in play here that you may not recognize or appreciate now. But as you keep reading, we'll unpack strategies and tactics that can change your relationships and outcomes with all the stakeholders in your personal and professional success. You're going to click "Send" dozens or hundreds of times this week as you reach out to these people. Each send is an opportunity to experience the big difference a simple video can make. Soon, you'll understand why—and what to do about it.

Everything you're going to learn was learned through years of our own use of video and years of working closely with community members in this personal video movement. What kinds of roles are they in?

- Inside sales
- Outside sales
- Customer service, support, and success
- Account-based marketing
- Account management
- Leadership and management
- Recruiting and talent development
- Business consulting and coaching
- Real estate, mortgage, and title services
- Financial planning and advising
- Automotive sales
- Insurance sales
- Network marketing
- Nonprofit fundraising and programming
- Entrepreneurship
- Teaching and education
- Speaking, music, entertainment
- More roles that delight and surprise us every day

If you teach, train, sell, or serve in any capacity, video can help you reach your desired outcomes faster, because it leads with your strongest asset . . . you. No matter where you fall on the Myers-Briggs, DISC, Birkman, Enneagram, or any other personality assessment, *who* you are matters. You're the difference-maker. Everything you've achieved so far has been achieved with and through other people based on your personality, expertise, and other qualities difficult to capture and convey in the typed-out messages you rely on every day. You're uniquely qualified to rehumanize your business.

VIDEO FOR RELATIONSHIPS, NOT JUST FOR MARKETING

When most people think of "video" in a business context, they think of scripts, lighting, casting, equipment, editing, postproduction, and other polishing touches that require a significant investment of time and money. We call this "marketing through video"—traditional video that's created in the style of a television commercial or a movie trailer. And this is a perfectly valid and useful effort. Videos with a long shelf life, wide audience, or high profile can provide a return on that investment in a "professional" production. For any person or company committed to marketing through video, keep going!

The personal video revolution drops the gloss and polish and capitalizes on video for its communication value in a no-fuss way. You smile, hit "Record," and talk to each person as if you're leaving a voicemail. You don't need a script for a voicemail. And you don't need any special equipment to say, "Thank you," "Nice to meet you," "Here's an update," "Happy birthday," or another message in this more personal way. You need only what you already have: a smartphone or a webcam, along with a message that's delivered better in person than in plain, typed-out text. You can see the difference with just a glance at Figure 1.3.

FIGURE 1.3 Marketing through Video versus Relationships through Video

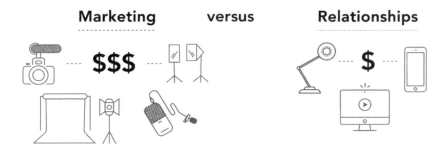

We call this type of communication "relationships through video." By losing all the extras, the video doesn't just *feel* more authentic—it *is* more authentic. It's you . . . a person we can look in the eye, hear out, and connect with despite the time and distance between us. You're communicating as if you're sitting across the table over coffee or lunch. And, like that experience, there are no do-overs—you just record and send. It's warmer and more complete than a typed-out message. It's faster and easier than writing, producing, and editing a video. And it's a return to the way humans have exclusively communicated for thousands and thousands of years—eye to eye, face to face.

The simple video style can be used in a variety of ways. Nearly every social network now has native video features that allow you to record or upload videos. YouTube, Snapchat, Facebook Live, Facebook Messenger, Facebook posts, LinkedIn posts, Instagram Stories, Instagram's IGTV— and that's just a short list of places people are hosting, posting, and sharing simpler videos. Though you'll be able to apply what we explore and explain to video in social posts, it's even more applicable to videos in text messaging and social messaging. Posts are broadcast. Messaging is personal.

Personal video can be used in emails, text messages, and social messages.

You might be thinking: *This approach seems insufficiently professional. Too casual. Too informal.* And you can find people who share this opinion. The irony is that these qualities are *exactly* why it's so effective. It's imperfect and makes you more approachable. Personal videos are more honest than marketing videos. When a video opens up with flashy, whooshy animation and stylized graphics, the viewer's guard goes up against a production that's designed to sell something. When a video opens up with a smiling face, a little wave, and a greeting to you by name, your guard goes down and you're drawn in by natural human connection.

If you've never done video, you can start with relationships through video. If you're marketing through video, you should layer in this personal style and equip your team members to do the same.

IT'S LIKE WE'VE ALREADY MET

As my coauthor Steve walked down a Chicago street, he heard his name shouted from across five lanes of traffic.

"Steve Pacinelli!" the person called out.

"Charlie Foxworth!" Steve shouted back.

Even though they'd never met in person or even spoken over the phone, Charlie felt enough confidence and enough connection to shout over to Steve. Even though he'd only "met" him through webcam videos, Steve recognized Charlie's face, recalled his name, and excitedly returned the greeting from 25 yards away. Years later, Charlie still tells that story. He recently shared it on a panel discussion that Steve moderated at a leadership conference. That moment years earlier clearly left a huge impression on Charlie and it was only possible because they had built their relationship through video. It was like they'd already met.

When I approached Andy Alger from across the room that day, it felt as if we'd already met, too. In the moment, I wasn't clear whether or not we *had* ever met face to face. This is something I've experienced with many other customers, too. In these moments, we smile, hug like longtime friends, then take a moment to establish whether or not we'd ever *actually* met in person. This happened with Ryan Shields, a sales professional from Brandon, Manitoba. By the time Ryan and I met in person the first time, I'd sent and received videos, written about him and his wife Jenn in our blog, told the story of the couple's journey into video success in a training course, and connected on a couple of social networks. When we finally connected face to face, it felt as if we'd already met. Further, it seemed unlikely that we *hadn't*.

One of the most consistent pieces of positive feedback we hear from people using video this way is that their recipients "feel like we've already met" when they initially meet in person. Leads, prospects, referrals, and other people with whom initial contact is digital are best greeted personally. These days, "digital" increasingly means visual, but for the past decade, direct communication's been all text all the time. Putting a face with your name in a personal video provides a stark and wonderful contrast to the standard . . . plain text.

VIDEO MAKES YOU MORE FAMILIAR AND APPROACHABLE

Building relationships through video isn't limited to one-to-one videos in emails, text messages, and social messages. It's not even limited to simple, casual videos. For decades, people sat in their living rooms and formed relationships with local television news anchors and weatherpeople, with game show hosts, and with fictional characters. That psychological connection is bred through frequency of exposure and creates a level of familiarity that brings us back night after night, week after week, episode after episode.

Prior to joining BombBomb, I spent nearly a dozen years running marketing teams inside local NBC, ABC, and FOX television stations. Our on-air talent often went out to live events like parades and festivals where viewers could meet them in person. Most who approached to connect and converse knew how long they'd been watching and offered one or two specific reasons they watched that anchor, reporter, or weatherperson. Many approached them as celebrities—with a degree of awe. Others, though, approached as if they were longtime, personal friends. These viewers shared deep and detailed stories about specific experiences watching that news or weather person on television.

Whether it's a Tina Fey sighting on the Upper West Side or a local news anchor sighting in the produce section of your neighborhood grocery store, we often experience a moment of "Hey, isn't that . . ." And this same familiarity is happening for normal, everyday people who are sending videos in order to communicate. Not for putting on a video "persona," but for being who they are. They're making themselves more approachable by getting face to face at scale. By humanizing their messages, processes, and businesses, they're no longer faceless email signatures and voicemails. They're familiar people.

As someone who's sent more than 8,000 videos in email and as someone who's embedded hundreds of videos in company blog posts, I've enjoyed dozens of customer conversations that I'd *never* have had otherwise. This happens most often at trade shows and starts with "Hey, Ethan," or "Hey, BombBomb guy," whether I'm standing in line for coffee, walking into a keynote session, or riding an elevator back up to my hotel room. And it happens whether or not I'm wearing an event badge with my name or wearing a company logo. It happens even more for Steve, who's not only sent thousands of videos but who's also delivered more than a thousand stage presentations.

More and better conversations as a consequence of sending video isn't restricted to in-person meetings. When I sent a personal video reply to one of our customers yesterday, I got a video email back with the subject line, "You are the MAN!!! Thanks for responding to me personally, I have finally arrived Ethan :)" A four-year customer, Connor MacIvor had sent more than 2,500 videos himself and was excited to have a personal video exchange with someone he felt like he knew by watching my videos over the years. It feels good to get a reply like that, and it feels great to share mutual respect with a customer through video.

This commitment to replacing some of your text with video creates a sense of familiarity that can function like minor fame or celebrity within your own network. This dynamic is often an excuse people make *not* to record videos. They think it's egocentric or begs "Hey, look at me." Just like any other piece of communication, though, video isn't about you unless you *make* it about you. If you're a humble servant, you come across as a humble servant in your videos. If you're a selfish egocentrist, that will come across, too.

Personal video should be rooted in customer empathy and consistent delivery of value. You become more recognizable, approachable, and connected in the process.

THE NUMBERS: VIDEO EMAIL VERSUS TRADITIONAL EMAIL

We've received countless anecdotes about the benefits of mixing personal videos into day-to-day business communication. In fact, I just received one from salesperson Justin Doornbos. Preparing for a speaking engagement, Justin reached out to the event coordinator for details, so he could book his flights and hotel. The response to the relatively unremarkable webcam video he recorded in his office: "OMG that is the BEST email I have honestly EVER received! I mean no joke. It made me smile and I will give you any agenda you need! Wow! Totally made my day!" And later in their email exchange: "That was the best email I have ever received and I get plenty of emails each day."

What was the coordinator trying to do with the ALL CAPS and exclamation points? She was trying to give back the positive energy and enthusiasm Justin delivered in his video simply by being himself. We get some version of this "more and better replies and responses" story all the time. So we sought to quantify the benefit based on that feedback. We asked people who have sent at least 10 videos what improvements they received from video email compared to traditional email. Here's what the nearly 500 participants reported:

81% get more replies and responses
87% get more clicks through their emails
68% have increased lead conversion
90% stay in touch more effectively
56% generate more referrals
One in six doubled or *more than* doubled their reply rate
One quarter doubled or *more than* doubled their click rate
One in 10 doubled or *more than* doubled their conversion rate
One in four doubled or *more than* doubled their ability to stay in touch
One in 10 doubled or *more than* doubled their referrals
Overall, 77% of people surveyed told us that video improved their results compared to text and 20% doubled their results.[1]

When we ran the same survey specifically for people recording, sending, and tracking video emails directly inside their Gmail inboxes through our Google Chrome extension, the results were similar, but higher across the board.

84% get more replies and responses
90% get more clicks through their emails
71% increased lead conversion
92% stay in touch more effectively
53% generate more referrals[2]

We also collected verbatim feedback in the survey to understand more specifically how and why they reported the lift. Here are some comments from coast to coast.

" I'm in the relationship business so my messaging through video has made a HUGE difference in my business and in the responses I receive!"

—

BRADENTON, FLORIDA

"I use video to follow up with my remote coaching clients after our calls. I think it really helps for them to see my smile and hear my voice, and so even if they never come to Durham, they feel like they know me, and in turn can trust me. Plus, being able to track my open and click-through rate is very helpful."

—

DURHAM, NORTH CAROLINA

"Video is personal and a big part of my business. It instills trust and builds relationship quicker. It can also save time, as people will know if they want to work with you or not. My smile is my brand but doesn't convey well in a simple email. It's also different than all other salespeople who've not even figured this out yet. Plus, I enjoy it!"

—

BARRIE, ONTARIO

"I've been able to close some fairly large and important deals, and I've been able to get the attention of some fairly high-level authority figures (in my world, anyway) that otherwise would have been very difficult to communicate with. Video has made a huge difference in my ability to communicate in an effective and engaging way that gets real, tangible results."

GRAND RAPIDS, MICHIGAN

"It allows me to communicate with people and it feels more personal because they see my face. When I meet them in person, I notice they are so much more relaxed in themselves than if I did a normal email. We sent videos while we were doing missions overseas and were able to show our supporters exactly where we were and the kids we were interacting with. It made fundraising overseas so much easier. Now I use it a lot to communicate with coworkers and to get RSVPs for events."

PARKER, COLORADO

" It's all about building trust with people you don't know or don't know very well. Personal video has the ability to cut through the clutter and noise consumers are bombarded with and puts a face and a voice with a name."

—

LA JOLLA, CALIFORNIA

" Video gives me a fantastic way to stay connected, to solidify relationships, and to build new ones because of the eye-to-eye conversation. Since using video, I have become one of the top recruiters in my company and I absolutely can say 100% that personal video plays a role in that. My customers appreciate the personal messages!"

—

HUNTINGTON BEACH, CALIFORNIA

> **"**Video has provided me with the ability to make clients and potential clients feel important and that I care. I recently had coffee with a client who recently was promoted to Executive Director of the nonprofit where he began as a part time worker. He shared with me that he got many messages of congratulations. The one that meant the most to him was my video email. It made him feel important because in the midst of my busy travel schedule I took the time to send him a personal message. When watching the video, he felt like I was talking to him live in person.**"**

FEDERAL WAY, WASHINGTON

The themes are obvious. This new way to communicate, connect, and convert is more personal than the status quo's faceless messages. Simple video builds trust and relationships. This is the foundation for sales acceleration and better customer experience.

THE STATS, CLAIMS, AND HYPE TO IGNORE

Over the years, we've seen all kinds of hyperbolic statistics about video come and go. I've even cited one or two of them myself (I blame youthful ignorance). The use of these stats and claims is like the use of inflammatory political memes on Facebook in that they don't serve anyone well and hinder substantial, meaningful conversation. So, let's go beyond the hype . . .

A Minute of Video Is *Not* Worth 1.8 Million Words

The trope goes like this: if a picture is worth a thousand words and a video is 30 frames per second, then video is like 30,000 words per second. This book contains a mere tens of thousands of words—let's say it's 60,000 words long. If a minute of video was worth 1.8 million words, we'd be able to deliver the entirety of the contents of this book to you in two seconds of video. That's ridiculous.

Video Does *Not* Produce a 200–300% Increase in Click-through Rate

This one is still being trotted out after making an appearance in a 2008 Forrester report. Rather than being an actual, measured result, it's completely anecdotal. I used it back in 2009 when there were no real stats and few real video email practitioners. There's absolutely no reason to use it today. Expect increases in engagement when you use video, but don't expect a tripling or quadrupling unless you're adding the video play itself to your other link clicks. Video provides human connection, not magic.

It Doesn't Matter That 82% of All Consumer Internet Traffic Will Be Video

The Cisco forecast that 82% of all consumer internet traffic will be video is solid, but using this statistic as an argument that you should be using video is foolish. Video is dramatically larger in file size than audio, photos, and graphics, which are dramatically larger in file size than text. As the image quality of videos continues to improve, gaps in traffic volume will grow even larger as it'll require even more bandwidth. Further, video's share of consumer internet traffic is driven far more by binging all nine seasons of *The Office* on Netflix, crushing hours of *FailArmy* videos on YouTube, and hosting billions of hours of commercial and residential security video recordings than it is by sending thousands of 52-second videos to prospects, customers, and team members.

Your Communication May Be 93% Nonverbal

You see this statistic on nonverbal communciation everywhere, not just around the topic of video. It comes from a flawed interpretation of two studies by UCLA Professor Emeritus of Psychology Albert Mehrabian with Morton Wiener and Susan Ferris in the late 1960s. In the "liking" or positive effects of a spoken message, 55% is attributed to facial cues, 38% to vocal qualities, and just 7% to the words themselves. Among the flaws of the statistics on spoken messages and the way they are popularly used are the following:

- This 55/38/7 split was produced by blending the results of two separate studies.

- In Mehrabian's own words, "Numerical values in this equation are only approximate."[3]
- Participants were all female; only half of our population was represented, and only a small group of women.
- Instead of being included in the context of a phrase, sentence, or real conversation, words were spoken individually; the women were reacting to just a single, spoken word like "brute" and "maybe," delivered in 15 different emotional tones. This was an artificial setting.
- Current research designed specifically to get at the humanizing effects of face and voice rather than text alone assigns equal or greater weight to voice.[4]

There's much to be learned from Mehrabian's work, but the takeaway that the words you choose don't matter very much *isn't* one of them. You don't need misinterpreted and misused research findings to know that your face and voice make your messages more effective.

Don't get confused or excited by claims being thrown around about video in your business. It's as simple as this: if you want to restore a human element to your business, if you want to save time by talking instead of typing, and if you want to build real relationships even when you can't get together in person, personal video as we've pioneered it with and through our customers is for you.

THE ONE QUESTION TO ASK YOURSELF

This style of video requires no production budget, special equipment, or specialized skills. You may be using videos on your website, in blog posts, in social media, and in other places, but this book isn't about broadcasting to large audiences and racking up anonymous video plays. We'll cover the basics of creating videos, but we won't reveal the secrets to becoming a zillionaire "YouTuber" or a paid Instagram "influencer."

What's unique here and what we're focused on are simple webcam and smartphone videos recorded and sent directly to the people who matter most to the success of your business or organization. These videos aren't to be compared to produced, polished, or "professional" videos. Instead, the proper point of comparison is the plain text you'd otherwise rely on to communicate that message.

So, the question to ask before you next click "Send" on a faceless message is, *Would I be more effective if I looked my customer or colleague in the eye and communicated with a personal video?*

CHAPTER 2

Email: The Indispensable, Broken Tool

At the turn of the millennium, email was great. We didn't receive very many emails and we appreciated each and every one we received. Open rates? Through the roof! The senders? People we knew personally—mom, uncle, sister, friend, colleagues, and companies we had well-established relationships with. "You've got mail!" sang AOL, reinforced by the impossibly charming 1998 film starring Tom Hanks and Meg Ryan. Remember that? I know it's distant. I know it's got the romanticism in which hindsight's often wrapped. But email was pretty great.

"YOU'VE GOT MAIL"

A romantic connection to email today? Not so much. One estimate has American workers spending one third of their work time in the inbox. That's at least 17 hours every week for the 40% of us with 50-hour workweeks.[1] A survey of 1,500 highly educated Canadian workers found that they spend 11.7 hours at work and 5.3 hours at home on email each week. They receive more than 120 emails per day and about half are regarded as spam.[2] Which generation spends the most time on email? Millennials, by far, at 6.4 hours per day.[3] If you work in a professional capacity, you use email. Often.

Even though we complain of being overwhelmed, nearly half of us report *electively* checking our work email outside normal work hours and more than half of us check personal email while we're at work. A survey of more than 1,000 white-collar American workers found that 27% of us check work email while having coffee, eating breakfast, or getting ready in the morning. Ahead of them: the 23% who check work email more while *still in bed!*[4] In total, we open 77% of work email and 59% of personal email. How do we feel about it all? Though we're occasionally excited by personal email (34%) and work email (17%), we're largely indifferent about both. We could fill an entire chapter with stats like these, but you already know it intuitively. You can't resist the draw of the inbox, even when it seems like too much. Relationship status: "It's complicated."

Volume's up and relevance is down. Spam makes up 45% of all emails sent and costs businesses an estimated $20.5 billion per year in lost productivity and technical expenses.[5] Yes, that's the fortune that awaits you via a Nigerian prince or the overseas executor of your long-lost family member's estate. And it's the unsolicited offer for pills, faceless request for connections on referral platforms, and pitch for services for which we've never been in the market. But it's not just the obvious stuff our increasingly smart spam filters snag for us. We spam each other. Ever been trapped in "Reply All" hell on topics unrelated to your role and responsibilities? Or in a seemingly ceaseless back-and-forth with another person that rivals the best Ping-Pong volley of all time and that could have been settled with a five-minute meeting?

Learn four ways to manage your inbox more effectively: BombBomb.com/BookBonus

Whether you scratch and claw toward Inbox Zero or proudly share screenshots of your 21,347 unread emails, find something that works for you, but don't take a victim's mindset about it. Be intentional and create a healthy relationship with your inbox—because it's not about the inbox, it's about your fellow humans on the sending and receiving ends of those messages.

ALTERNATIVES TO EMAIL

So, what's the answer to our email ambivalence? Automation? It can work, but only in well-defined and highly repetitive processes. We can write rules to manage the inbox, have our email sorted and prioritized for us, and have replies sent on our behalves. Automated email saves senders time and improves productivity. With Conversica, our company sets up triggered sends and sequences to help prospects and customers schedule appointments with our human team members. When specific criteria are met, the sequence starts. When a recipient replies, Conversica can read key words and sentiments and respond accordingly.

Enhancing tools and systems like this one with *adaptive* automation makes them better with every send through artificial intelligence and machine learning. Bot sends and replies are full of promise and already delivering results, but an inbox that runs itself is not yet available to you and me. Digital pals like Siri, Alexa, Cortana, and Google Assistant can fetch things for you, answer questions, help you shop, take dictation, read to you, and recommend words or phrases for message responses, but they're not quite ready to run your inbox.

How about something like the collaborative messaging app Slack? The promise is made in headlines like "How Slack Is Killing Email," "Using Slack at Work? Here's How to Reduce Email by 80% or More," and "Slack app: How this company will kill email and change the way we work." Yes! Let's kill the beast . . . by moving all those messages into a new channel that has added and often exaggerated urgency, inflated expectations of immediate reply, increased likelihood of "reply all" irrelevance, and increased attention demand as alerts tally up and fly onto our screens incessantly.

Steve and I use Slack every day; our entire company does. It's an extremely useful tool to communicate with team members, close partners and suppliers, and groups of like-minded people who join themed channels, but it doesn't save time or preserve attention. It offers some great features and functions that our inboxes don't, but the reality is a both/and situation with Slack and email. Or any messaging app and email.

Social networks and social messaging? We've moved many of our conversations there, but not the majority of them. For better and for worse, they're less formal than more traditional communication channels. One key weakness is inconsistency. You're connected to him on Facebook and Twitter. You're connected to her only on LinkedIn. And you're connected to them on Facebook, Instagram, *and* LinkedIn. But those two guys don't respond to LinkedIn messages, even though she does—but only a couple of times a week. Lack of consistency makes it hard to loop in everyone involved in a project, process, or transaction in a single social channel. Social messaging is best on a person-by-person basis after someone's proven a presence in and preference for it.

Texting? 81% of the American population has access. 97% of smartphone users sent a text in the past week. And the open rate is 99%.[6] Even with automated appointment reminders, it's still an intimate place. Because of this, it's more commonly used in a B2C relationship than in a B2B situation— at least until a close relationship's been built. A sole practitioner or small business owner is more likely to text directly with people than a mid-market or enterprise company's inside sales and customer service reps.

Phone calls? We've aged out of the golden "You've got calls!" era. More than 3 billion robocalls go out every month.[7] Fraudulent calls grew from 3.7% of mobile phone calls in 2017 to 29.2% in 2018. They're projected to climb to 44.6% of all calls in 2019.[8] In other words, spam calls to your mobile phone will be equal to or *greater than* spam emails sent to your inbox! At the same time, spoofing technologies are getting better and better, too, so the fraudulent calls keep getting through. At least the spam filter for your email has decades of experience and machine learning behind it. Unless your number's been added as a known contact, your odds of someone picking up your call are slim.

Video conferencing and video chat? They overcome distance. Any two people with a camera and an internet connection can get face to face from anywhere in the world. It's the next best thing to being there in person. But they don't overcome time, because they're synchronous. You've both got to be available at the same time. And in a professional context, it should be scheduled. You know that back-and-forth:

"Sorry I didn't make the call at 3 p.m., I got the time zones mixed up."
"Are you available on Thursday at 9 a.m. or 11 a.m.?"
"No, how about next Tuesday afternoon?"

When you send an email or video email, you do it when it works for you. Your recipient may look at it immediately, later that morning, or sometime in the next couple days—when it works for him or her. Asynchronicity adds convenience for both sender and receiver. And tracking closes the loop, so you know when they opened your email and played your video.

So, the answer's not either/or, it's both/and. These alternatives are all part of the fragmentation of communication. When conversations start in the email inbox, they may migrate out to another channel. But email may remain primary, even as you mix in video conferencing, phone calls, or social messaging. In the words of a great email we recently received from Copy Hackers, "In the digital marketing world, email is as close to immortal as it comes."

THE INDISPENSABLE TOOL

Email remains ubiquitous; it's still the go-to business communication platform. It's withstood tests of time and thrived in the face of threats from all comers. We all use email every day. Many of us use it multiple times or even perpetually throughout the day. We're closing in on 4 billion email users worldwide—more than half the world's population.[9] Gmail alone claims more than a quarter of those users. Most of us have more than one email address; we average 1.75 addresses per user. And though the growth rate has slowed to 3% a year, that rate of growth on billions produces increases in the tens of millions of people.

For more than a dozen years, email marketing's remained the top digital channel for return on investment. The Direct Marketing Association and Demand Metric recently reported a median ROI of 122% for email—more than four times higher than social media, direct mail, and paid search.[10] Email's ROI is described as "excellent" to "good" by 74% of companies.[11] And it's been this way for years. On the consumer side, we still choose email over direct mail, social, texting, and phone calls as the preferred way to hear from brands at 50% (versus 20%, 7%, 7%, and 7%, respectively).[12]

Great, but that's mostly about email marketing and sales prospecting. What about direct email communication? Per HubSpot, 86% of professionals prefer to use email when communicating for business purposes. On the consumer (and youth) side, Adestra found that 68% of teens and 73% of millennials prefer to receive communication from a business through email, 86% use their smartphones for email, and 48% of teens and 44% of millennials do so *immediately* upon waking up in the morning.[13] Per that same study, face-to-face communication and email are tied as our most preferred work communication channel (31%), but we use email more often (72% to 61%). We can pile up more and more reference points, but the fact remains that despite fragmentation into other channels and despite it being the method that is longest in use, email's not going anywhere.

For its ease, familiarity, ubiquity, interoperability, targeting, trackability, and other winning characteristics, email remains a killer app. Instead of remaining faceless, however, email can easily be rehumanized in a way that saves you time and improves results—with personal videos.

THE PROBLEM OF (OVER)CRAFTING YOUR EMAILS

When we write emails, we labor over every word we type. And even though we expect we've done a good job making our message clear, we consistently *overestimate* our communication quality. Now an assistant professor in the Management Department at the McCombs School of Business at the University of Texas at Austin, Andrew Brodsky, PhD, was a doctoral candidate at Harvard Business School when he reached out to me about creating a research project. He'd already done several studies related to organizational behavior, work communication, and employee productivity and was curious about traditional email and video email.

From volunteers in the BombBomb customer base, mountains of data were collected about traditional emails, video emails, time spent, emotional effect, message effectiveness, and more. In the abstract of the third chapter of his dissertation, Andrew captured the true pain of traditional emails in this way: "In an experience sampling study, which captured email communication in real time, I find that workers will often engage in over-crafting of email, whereby workers spend extra time crafting messages to the detriment of their productivity, message effectiveness, and well-being."[14]

Many of those hours spent in our inboxes slow us down and wear us out as we work and overwork to organize the words in a way that gets our message through in the way we intend. But the inherent limitations of the medium and the limiting factor of our egos keep us short of the goal line. Effective communication in plain email is limited by the absence of gesture, emphasis, and tone. In the opening of a research piece titled "Egocentrism Over E-Mail: Can We Communicate As Well As We Think?," the authors summarize their findings: "Five experiments suggest that this limitation is often underappreciated, such that people tend to believe that they can communicate over email more effectively than they actually can."[15]

When you restrict yourself to typed-out text, the absence of nonverbal communication leaves your emails emotionally void and, therefore, more difficult to understand. As you labor through crafting the message, you know your intended meaning. You see it and hear it in the words you wrote, but your recipients may not. We're not as good at it as our egos tell us.

Something else your recipients may overlook is that you're a thinking, feeling human on the sending end of the message. A recent study subtitled "Voice Reveals the Presence of a Humanlike Mind" compared perceptions and consequences of text communication versus voice and video communication. A "fundamental" finding: when you rely on plain text to communicate with others, the effect is to dehumanize yourself in their minds. As listeners, we assign intention, emotion, and other human qualities to the speaker. As readers, however, we fail to associate the words on the screen with a thinking, feeling person. "Across six experiments, people who listened to natural speech (or actors mimicking natural speech) consistently believed communicators were more thoughtful, competent, agentic, and likable than people who read their speeches or read their writing."[16]

The authors acknowledge that a highly skilled writer may be able to humanize their writing but confirm that randomly selected readers don't "spontaneously humanize the text as they are reading." Listening is different. Voice is so humanizing that we even apply its benefits to our phones. In their study, people who used Siri on their iPhones saw it as more mindful, intelligent, responsive, friendly, and sophisticated than smartphone users who didn't use the voice feature. We have more positive impressions of messages delivered by people we can see or even just hear. We have greater empathy toward the communicator when we can see or hear him or her. Intergroup conflict and prejudice often begin by dehumanizing "them" or the "others"; social conflict is more effectively managed by restoring "their" faces and voices.

Hiding behind a cloak of digital anonymity, cyberbullying, trolling, and igniting flame wars online is the theme of an important opinion piece published in the *New York Times*. In "The Epidemic of Facelessness," writer Stephen Marche connects the absence of the human face to significant communication and behavior problems. He draws on Plato's 2,400-year-old myth about the Ring of Gyges, which makes its wearer invisible at will, to illustrate the disinhibiting effects of not being seen and the corrupting effects of anonymity. Today, the Gyges effect is used to describe these monstrous behaviors of "keyboard warriors" who hide behind the screen as they say things they'd *never* say if they had to look the person on the other end of their cyberbullying or trolling in the eye.

The resolve is clear. "As communication and exchange come at a remove, the flight back to the face takes on a new urgency," writes Marche.[17] Whether in sales, marketing, support, project management, or any other role, you can't afford to continue relying exclusively on faceless digital communication. We need to rehumanize our communication and our businesses.

SO, EMOJIS?

An emoji or emoticon may have a "face," but it's an insufficient replacement for a smiling human. If you get especially friendly with your customers or clients, you may add emojis to your business communication. Over the days, weeks, or months of a B2C sales process that starts a customer lifecycle, the relationship may reach that level of comfort, familiarity, and informality. But not every client or client relationship is the same.

If instead you're in B2B enterprise sales and trying to close a six-, seven-, or even eight-figure deal, it's unlikely that the SVP or C-level executive will accept your crying, laughing, round yellow "faces" as useful and professional expressions – at least not until the relationship is well established. Your truth likely falls somewhere in between these two examples, but you should know your recipient before dropping an emoticon as a substitute for your absent, human face.

We add emojis to make clearer the intention of our words and to add a little personality or flair. Are you serious or are you joking? Punch in that smiley face. But which smiley face does your recipient get? And do they read it the same way you do? Different operating systems often "speak" different emojis and different people often interpret the same emoji differently. The authors of a study titled "'Blissfully Happy' or 'Ready to Fight': Varying Interpretations of Emoji" found that only 4.5% of emoji symbols examined "have consistently low variance in their sentiment interpretations. Conversely, in 25% of the cases where participants rated the same rendering, they did not agree on whether the sentiment was positive, neutral, or negative."[18]

In other words, emojis and emoticons don't make things clear; they add to the misunderstandings. But that hasn't slowed their use. As they become more common, they become more acceptable. Still, they can't compete with human, nonverbal cues for context, clarity, meaning, intention, or connection.

REPAIRING EMAIL

While our communication fragments across email, text messaging, messaging apps, social messaging, social networks, or other channels, we're still restricting our most important and most valuable messages to plain text far more often than not. Most of your communication and exchange comes "at a remove," to use Marche's words. Well intentioned or not, you often don that cloak of digital anonymity. You're hiding behind the same black text on the same white screen, even though you've got a lot riding on your messages' outcomes. There's a new urgency to repairing email – to making "the flight back to the face."

> There's a new urgency to restoring a critical, missing element . . . you!

Whether you're teaching, training, or selling, you add so much meaning and value to your communication. As you'll soon understand clearer than ever, people *need* to see you. Trust and rapport. Attention and understanding. Accuracy and transparency. These are all achieved faster and more effectively when you make the flight back to the face.

CHAPTER 3

Video: The Personal, Rehumanizing Tool

"I see you." In the 2009 film *Avatar*, a huge box office and critical success, the Na'vi greeted each other with these words. The words mean that you're present and attentive—that you're completely open and welcoming to the other person . . . or sentient humanoid, in the case of the Na'vi. We need to see each other. And we have a deep need to be seen. The literal and emotional aspects of seeing and being seen are fundamental to the human experience. When used to build personal and professional relationships, video helps us see and be seen.

RELATIONSHIPS ARE THE WHOLE POINT

The Grant Study began at Harvard more than 80 years ago with the goal of discovering how to live a long, healthy, and fulfilling life. Initial participants in the longitudinal study were 238 Harvard sophomores. Over the years, the participant groups expanded to include inner-city Boston residents and the original participants' children, at which point it became the Grant and Glueck Study. The researchers considered various factors and data, including career, financial, social, intelligence, genetic, mental, physical, and other types of measures.

Across several populations, across decades, and across criteria, the greatest predictor of health was consistent: our relationships with other people. Robert Waldinger, the study's director, a professor of psychiatry at Harvard Medical School, and the source of one of the most popular TED talks of all time describes the study's "revelation" in this way: "The surprising finding is that our relationships and how happy we are in our relationships has a powerful influence on our health."[1]

Our personal success, life satisfaction, and well-being are enabled through the people in our lives. And so is our business success. As Gary Vaynerchuk offered in the opening to his book *The Thank You Economy*, "No relationships should be taken for granted. They are what life is all about, the whole point. How we cultivate our relationships is often the greatest determinant of the type of life we get to live. Business is no different."[2] The personal/professional connection is also offered in *The Go-Giver*, a classic from Bob Burg and John David Mann: "A genuinely sound business principle will apply anywhere in life – in your friendships, in your marriage, anywhere. That's the true bottom line." This was offered in support of their Law of Authenticity, which states that "the most valuable gift you have to offer is yourself."[3]

So, connecting and communicating with others improves our lives and our businesses. We do this best when we're present with others. We do it best in person, face to face. Think about the people involved in your personal and professional success: family and friends, team members and recruits, prospects and customers, suppliers and partners. Think about all the people who help make your achievements possible.

In terms of connecting and communicating with these people, are you more effective in a typed-out email or text message, or are you more effective on the phone?

Most people say they're better on the phone. Voice, pace, and tone allow you to express yourself more clearly. And the feedback loop—the give and take of a conversation—creates a much richer experience for both people. Any two people anywhere in the world with a phone and an internet, cellular, or landline connection can enjoy this experience, no matter the distance. You just need to coordinate the time (and the time zones!).

Similar question, but with a new option: Are you more effective on the phone or more effective in person?

Nearly everyone says they're more effective in person. Take all the benefits of talking over the phone, but add in face, posture, body language, distance, eye contact, hand gestures, and all those rich, nonverbal cues that our brains are wired to receive from one another. We're fellow human beings. We're social creatures. Because of the subtlety, nuance, emotion, energy, and all those little things that just don't come through our typed-out or spoken words alone, we're better in person. A deep history and millennia of evolution have refined this wiring.

We need to see each other. Sending personal video helps fulfill that need when time and distance get in your way.

MILLENNIA OF HUMAN BRAIN TRAINING

As a species, humans have been speaking to one another for about 150,000 years. There's a great debate about this number; estimates range from 50,000 years to more than one million years, well before our evolution into homo sapiens.[4] You can imagine the difficulty in figuring that out. Early symbols and writing can be found; the materials' dates of the origin can be established. It's far more challenging to determine when we started speaking to each other. There's no record of a spoken word—not prior to our ability to record audio, anyway. We have to infer from indirect data the ability, hence the debate. Rather than get into the debate's particulars, though, we'll work from the conservative end of the range—150,000 years. Most of that time, we've spoken to our fellow humans exclusively face to face. Only in the past handful of generations could we record and transmit our faces and voices across time and distance using technology.

Our brains have more than 100,000 years of experience, training, and refinement in spoken, face-to-face communication.

So, how long have humans been writing? The oldest known cave paintings in Chauvet Cave in southern France date back 30,000 years to the Ice Age or Upper Paleolithic era.[5] Twelve thousand years is the age of the oldest known pictograph, "an early method of writing in which pictures are used to convey meaning—similar to hieroglyphics."[6] Five thousand years ago, the transition from capturing visual images in paintings and drawings to capturing speech sounds in writing was made by the Sumerians of Mesopotamia. Called cuneiform, this form of writing evolved from a symbol-based accounting system into a system of phonetic symbols. Over the next several hundred years, the Sumerians developed it into a purer alphabet that was eventually used to capture poems and literature.[7] Egyptian hieroglyphics also date back to this period and possessed some of the uniformity of an early form of alphabet.

Writing's evolution is richer and more nuanced than conveyed here, but the point should be clear. We've only been writing for about 5,000 years – one thirtieth or 3.3% of the amount of time we've been speaking to one another. The true ratio of writing to speaking is even smaller than that, though. How much smaller? Add a zero and make it *one three hundredth,* or 0.3%, because nearly that entire time the vast majority of the human population was illiterate. Literacy rates only started spreading into the population at large—unevenly, of course—about 500 years ago.[8]

Only 500 years of widespread reading and writing; this amount of time is too short to produce major evolutionary changes to master the complexity of producing and decoding strings of symbols (reading and writing text). The gap between 150,000 and 500 is made obvious in Figure 3.1. Scientists are only starting to understand the relationship between the brain circuits used for reading and writing and those used for seeing and speaking, but one study's authors gracefully observe that "a preliterate brain must adapt on the fly, so to speak, in learning how to process written words, rather than being able to rely upon evolutionarily ancient modifications of the visual system pathways."[9]

This explains why we struggle to craft effective emails and overestimate our ability to do so; reading and writing is adapted. This also explains why restoring the messenger to the message with video is so effective; seeing and speaking

FIGURE 3.1 History of Human Speech, Writing, and Literacy

are ancient. We've been communicating with one another face to face for approximately *300 times longer* than we've been communicating through written words. It's more natural and fundamentally human.

When you're hiring a new salesperson, you're not likely assigning a writing test as part of the employment screen. You're asking them to "sell me this pen" (come on, you know you've done it) and collecting a DISC assessment or Caliper profile to gain insights into a candidate's strengths, motivations, behavioral tendencies, and communication style. When you're hiring someone for the client care team, you're evaluating abilities to empathize, connect, defuse, and transform. You require competence in reading and writing, but you're not looking for a modern-day Jane Austen or William Shakespeare. You don't need Strunk or White. While putting J.K. Rowling or John Grisham on your outbounding team might win you some calls back, your new salesperson need not turn out a 200,000-word novel.

Instead of evaluating and hiring talent based on interpersonal skills and then hiding these professionals behind voicemails and typed-out emails, empower them with video.

After you land and onboard the best person, you tend to cloak them in emails and voicemails. You need to help your company's representatives shine. You need to unlock their potential and put them back into a true sales or service role. Empowering tvhem with video recording, sending, and tracking is a leap toward the rehumanization of your business.

OUR FACES SPEAK THE SAME LANGUAGE

While we struggle to produce competent writing in one of the thousands of written languages in use today, our faces all speak the same language. Human facial expression of emotion is both universal and innate. We all do it the exact same way – across societies, across cultures, and across history. There's a rich body of research built by different researchers at different universities and institutions using different methodologies and participants in different cities, countries, and continents. All conducted across different decades. And despite these differences, the work points to one key finding: human emotions are expressed the same way through our faces.

With the goal of surveying the best research on nonverbal behavior and making practical the key findings, the authors of *Nonverbal Communication: Science and Applications* describe facial expressions of emotion in this way: "The ability to read facial expressions of emotion can help your interactions with anyone regardless of his or her race, culture, ethnicity, nationality, sex, religion, or age."[10] Even when we speak to people through an interpreter, we understand what they're saying with their faces; it's universal.

The importance of this ability to read and write the same language through our faces alludes to its evolutionary depth. It helps us survive and thrive as healthy members of society. Reading others' emotions helps us accurately and reliably see a person's personality, motivations, and intentions. It helps us build rapport and relationship, as well as evaluate honesty and truth. Any effort that involves negotiation, persuasion, and influence benefits from this universal, human ability.

Human facial expression of emotion is also innate to us. We all do it from infancy. In as few as four months, a baby's brain can process and analyze faces at near-adult levels, according to recent psychology research at Stanford.[11] In contrast, most toddlers start speaking between 18 and 24 months and most children start reading between the ages of 5 and 7 years. As you see in Figure 3.2, infants read human faces in one twentieth the time they begin to read basic words. Further, infants' ability to recognize and read faces is prioritized over other skills; non-facial images and objects are analyzed at lower levels of our visual systems. Infants are extremely responsive to facial emotions; our social lives start early and begin with faces.

This is not learned behavior based in mimicry. Our ability to read and write emotions to our faces is nearly statistically identical when comparing expressions of blind and sighted people. This consistency is also observed in studies of twins and families, as well as reviews of developmental literature and analyses of nonhuman primates. One of the gifts of being human is that our faces all speak the same language and we don't have to learn how to do it. So, why are we hiding our faces so often in our professional lives? How much more successful might we be if we got face to face more often?

FIGURE 3.2 Human Development of Facial Recognition, Speech, and Reading

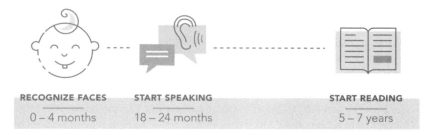

RECOGNIZE FACES	START SPEAKING	START READING
0 – 4 months	18 – 24 months	5 – 7 years

THE EYES HAVE IT

Latin for "Little Brain," the cerebellum is a primal and primarily subconscious region of the brain that's evolved over millions of years. It allows us to lock eyes on a moving target, as well as to communicate and connect both consciously and subconsciously.[12] Even brief eye contact with another person can trigger empathetic feelings and draw us closer together through the release of the neuropeptide hormone oxytocin (the "love hormone").[13] Humans are motivated, then, to make and maintain eye contact with one another.

This connection through the eyes can be so mentally stimulating that research has shown we have trouble performing other mental tasks while we're engaged in eye contact.[14] We're more likely to remember the face of a person with whom we've made eye contact and more likely to believe what he or she says to us.[15,16] Without eye contact, we perceive people to be less sincere and less conscientious.[17,18] Connection through the eyes is an important social and relational development for us; it's highly functional. As with the facial expressions of emotion, it runs deep in the human experience.

When recording videos, look the camera in the lens so that you're making eye contact with your viewer.

In those moments of eye contact is also a human connection, an ethical impulse, a spark of morality. French phenomenologist and Jewish philosopher Emmanuel Levinas wrote about the significance of "the eyes of the Other" and the face of the other.[19] Awareness of self is preceded by and only made possible through recognition of another person. As we look at another, we look at ourselves and at all of humanity. Through this, we gain a sense of obligation—an ethical and empathic impulse. We're obliged to return thoughts and behaviors in kind.

Face-to-face connection affects us meaningfully and even involuntarily. Direct eye contact inspires spontaneous mimicry of others, enhances affiliation with others, and improves social interaction. One study found evidence that a direct gaze "rapidly and specifically enhances mimicry of intransitive hand movements."[20] So, the eyes have it in both an immediate and an infinite way. And about those hand movements . . .

TALKING WITH YOUR HANDS

An analysis of thousands of hours of TED talks found that the most popular talks were delivered by people who made an average of 465 hand gestures. The least popular? About half as many gestures, at 272.[21] Our hands are tied to our use of language—both as speakers and listeners. They help us speak more clearly, quickly, and effectively. They help people pay attention, perceive the speaker as more passionate and enthusiastic, and understand more information. As extensions of our thoughts and emotions, our hand movements enhance our communication.[22]

In person and in video, keep your hands in front of you. Their absence can trigger feelings of distrust. Maintain fluid motion—natural and smooth, rather than robotic or abrupt. Palms open at a 45-degree angle conveys honesty and openness while palms down conveys confidence. Palms at 90 degrees facing each other and fingers closed together conveys expertise. When you clasp your hands or touch your neck, face, or hair, we see you as hesitant and unsettled.[23]

Some ways to use your hands in person and in video are the following:

- Conveying openness, confidence, or authority
- Listing and counting
- Enhancing the contrast between this and that
- Gesturing toward you or me
- Emphasizing sizes or quantities of things
- Bringing things together or sending them apart

Because our hands help communicate our messages, they increase the value of video. So do our posture and entire body. Social psychologist Amy Cuddy popularized the concept of power posing with her 2012 TED talk and 2015 book *Presence*. The main idea is that when you change your body's posture, you change your chemistry and behavior. Though there's been some academic debate about the effectiveness of power posing, we've successfully taught some of the techniques for use in video.

In an online training class, we asked dozens of people to record a video. Then, we taught them physically expansive and open "high-power" poses (for example, standing upright with hands on hips like Wonder Woman). We cautioned against physically contracting and closed "low-power" poses (for example, hunching or leaning inward with arms or legs crossed). Afterward, each person recorded a new video. Most of the new videos felt far more confident to both subject and viewer. Even if you don't intentionally pose, staying aware of your posture and body language should improve your on-camera and in-person presence.

To assure that your hands and more of your body appear in your videos, step back from the camera or move the camera away from you. This breaks you out of a tight head-and-shoulders shot and gives you a wider view that most people find more flattering. Few people like to see their faces fill the frame. An inability to see your own hands because of a tight shot can give you the awkwardness of Will Ferrell's "I'm not sure what to do with my hands" scene as Ricky Bobby in the 2006 comedy *Talladega Nights*. The scene was hilarious, but the struggle is real.

On business trips, we often rely on our laptop webcams from a hotel room for a video call or video email. Unless the laptop's set back, I feel like I'm in a tight box. Back at the office, though, a wider-angle webcam set up in the corner of the room opens things up dramatically and allows better nonverbal communication. And if you're using a smartphone, you might want to use (gasp!) a selfie stick to create a wider view than if you just held it out with your arm.

Get your hands into the frame from the top of your video by starting with a friendly wave, by briefly holding up a whiteboard, notecard, or notepad with a message, or by gesturing toward something in the room. From there, speak as comfortably as you would if you were at a social event or across the table over coffee. Use your upper body, including your hands, to express yourself. You'll be more comfortable, and your viewer will warm up to you quicker.

THE WARMTH OF YOUR SMILE

Another important idea advanced by many researchers working with the Stereotype Content Model, including Amy Cuddy, is how people judge us upon meeting us—whether in person, in video, or in typed-out text. They use two main criteria: warmth and competence. Warmth translates to trust, rapport, and relationship. In a sales context, it's their desire to work with you and the ease with which they say yes to you. Competence is your knowledge and expertise. It's your perceived ability to get the job done well.

The person with the best credentials, of course, doesn't always win. The person who *connects* most effectively often does. This is because even though people judge us on both criteria, warmth trumps competence. People need to know that you're going to use your competence with their best interests in mind, and warmth bridges that gap. In famous words attributed to Teddy Roosevelt, John Maxwell, and others, "People don't care how much you know until they know how much you care."

> Warmth is difficult to judge in text-based messages.

As shared in the previous chapter, people tend not to perceive you as a thinking, feeling person as they read the email you wrote. Personal videos, on the other hand, establish that you're a real person and warm up your relationships. One universally understood conveyance of warmth: the smile. Smiling provides many personal and professional benefits. Just as you want to make regular eye contact throughout a video or a lunch meeting, an occasional smile (especially at the start and close) helps you build trust and rapport. And it feels good. Smiling is a valuable and healthy habit.

Personal Benefits of a Smile
- Reduces stress (releases neuropeptides)
- Relaxes you and lowers blood pressure (releases dopamine, endorphins)
- Improves your mood (releases serotonin)

Professional Benefits of a Smile
- Makes others perceive you as more relaxed, attractive, warm
- Makes others more likely to believe you're a nice person
- Makes other more likely to comply with your requests[24]

Just as it's advised to "smile before you dial," smile before you hit "Record" to put yourself in a better mood and make a good first impression. When you can be yourself fully and express yourself naturally in simple videos, both your competence *and* your warmth come through.

OUTSMARTING OUR MENTAL SHORTCUTS

Why is video so much more effective than text for judgments of warmth? Among the many reasons is the dual theory of the mind. On one side are rationality, logic, reason, intellect, and thinking. On the other are irrationality, emotion, instinct, impulse, and feeling. This is a long-standing model that dates back to Plato's allegory of the chariot. The Greek philosopher described two horses, one of noble breed (logic) and the other of ignoble breed (emotion), pulling our minds forward. We struggle to keep them working together at a proper pace on the path to enlightenment.

In a contemporary context, Daniel Kahneman, one of the world's foremost behavioral economists and a Nobel Memorial Prize winner, captures the idea with System One and System Two in *Thinking, Fast and Slow*, one of the most well-received books of 2011. System One is gut, emotion, and instinct. It's the source of that good feeling about a person within a few seconds of meeting him or her. System One is thinking fast. Also in play is System Two, thinking slow. It's logic and reason. It takes more energy to crank through this mental processing. Because our brains are efficient, slow thinking is a slave to fast thinking. We make most decisions with System One. Projects get kicked up and assigned to System Two only out of need. And even then, our emotion and impulse are at the root.[25] Review the differences in Figure 3.3 before seeing the two systems at work in one of Steve's decisions.

When Steve bought a motorcycle, he shared with me his excitement about the great gas mileage he'd get compared to his car. He'd save some real money. What a great reason. So smart. Who doesn't want to save some money by increasing fuel efficiency? Of course, that logic didn't drive his decision. Instead, it was driven by emotion. He imagined the experience of letting loose out on winding, country roads. What a great feeling. So freeing. Who

FIGURE 3.3 The Dual Theory of the Mind

Dual Theory of the Mind

IGNOBLE	Noble
SYSTEM ONE	System Two
IRRATIONALITY	Rationality
EMOTION	Logic
INSTINCT	Reason
IMPULSE	Intellect
FEELING	Thinking
FAST	Slow
EASY	Laborious

doesn't want to enjoy the closest thing to flying without leaving the ground? He rationalized an emotional decision. Both of Kahneman's Systems are operating. Each of us is constantly riding Plato's chariot.

You may be thinking: *Fascinating. So what's this mean for my business communication?* As we work to inform and influence people, we often rely on plain text to get the job done. When someone receives your three-paragraph email or typed-out Facebook message, which system of thinking are you engaging? That's right: System Two (slow). Our minds labor as they parse through phrases, sentences, and paragraphs to discern your meaning, purpose, and opportunity. Yes, most people are capable of doing that, even if slowly or poorly. But it doesn't engage them in the way that serves both parties best.

We want to engage System One (fast) to give people that positive, gut feeling and to generate that instinctual "I like this person" reaction. We want to establish warmth before competence. Rehumanizing your business with personal videos restores the balance in how we engage people.

Do you know how many decisions we make every day? I don't, either. But it's not dozens or hundreds. We likely make tens of thousands of decisions daily. One widely cited number is 35,000. We start with things like whether to hit the snooze button on the alarm or get out of bed. A couple of hundred decisions are made each day just on what to eat. With all this mental activity, much of it done in the background without our immediate awareness, why aren't we completely exhausted within an hour of waking? Because our brains seek patterns, then create rules and shortcuts. Refined through millennia of training and development, our minds are highly efficient.

When you receive an email with an opening line wanting "just 15 minutes of your time," what's your first thought? Maybe, *Here comes the sales pitch!* or *More like 30 minutes, right?* This is pattern recognition, which we turn into mental shortcuts. Should we delete or engage? Dr. Robert Cialdini, professor of marketing, business, and psychology and author of *Influence*, *Yes!*, and *Pre-suasion*, describes this as "click-whirr" decision making.[26] The same stimuli produce the same responses because of shortcuts. I've received several hundred of these cold emails, so I recognize them, and the same goes with with LinkedIn connection requests. Too often, the company name, sales-related job title, overly friendly message, and lack of mutual connections work together to say one thing: "I'm going to direct-message you a sales pitch as soon as you accept this connection request." In weaker moments, I accept them anyway. And nine times out of 10, the mental shortcut I've created is validated . . . the sales pitch comes seconds later.

When you arrive in an inbox or text message with a smiling face, a friendly wave, and eye contact, you're breaking a pattern and violating an expectation. The medium itself is an unanticipated message. You're not sending another faceless request for "just 15 minutes" of someone's time. As Keenan, President, CEO, and Chief Antagonist of A Sales Guy Inc., describes in his book *Gap Selling*, you're "triggering the ACC," or the anterior cingulate cortex. This is the part of the brain that connects to both the "emotional" limbic system and "cognitive" prefrontal cortex.

Among other jobs, the ACC detects errors and monitors conflict; it constantly hunts for things that violate norms and expectations, then highlights and calls attention to them. It forces a judgment and decision. A message rehumanized with a personal video demands attention and action because it breaks a pattern.

> Mix up your message style and cadence to break mental patterns.

To outsmart our mental shortcuts, you need to be seen. And once you have that attention, your video improves communication, connection, and conversion. When you break up the email and voicemail pattern with a video, we have no predetermined path, so we're forced to engage with and evaluate your message. You're triggering our ACC, so we see you.

Instead of deleting another plain email because it fits the pattern, we're meeting you and assessing the opportunity you represent. We're weighing your warmth and your competence. We're subconsciously looking for signs of trust. You're helping us say yes. That yes may be a micro-conversion of replying or scheduling a call or it may be a macro-conversion of choosing you and signing a contract.

Personal video is rehumanizing. It helps you make Marche's "flight back to the face." It puts you, the messenger, back into your messages. In the words of the authors of *Nonverbal Communication: Science and Applications*: "Nonverbal communication adds nuance, shading, and depth of meaning to all communication, and strictly verbal media—email, text messaging—deprives us of most of that."[27] Video injects nonverbal information back into the media you and your team rely on every day. If you're still deciding whether video's a good fit for your business, we present six specific signs that indicate that you need it in the next chapter.

CHAPTER 4

———

Six Signs This New Approach Is for You and Your Business

I've sent thousands of videos for the purpose of teaching, training, connecting, serving, and selling. Many of those videos were sent to lists of people, but the vast majority have been personal. Within our community, nearly a thousand people have each sent a thousand videos or more. A handful have sent more than 5,000 videos. As I often say, you don't send your 5,000th video if the previous 4,999 weren't effective for you. And you don't send your 5,000th video if it's difficult or cumbersome.

You don't get to a thousand videos by mass sending. Even if you consistently sent one video every week to everyone on your team, in your company, in your database, or in your community, you'd only be at about 200 or 250 videos after five years, assuming you take a few weeks off every year. This rate and volume of simple video sending that we see and study is all about one-to-one messages—truly personal videos. If you're exclusively playing a volume game, this approach may not be for you. But if you value the relationship above the transaction because the initial touch is the start of a long, productive customer journey, you're in the right place.

Should you join these people by sending some of your most valuable messages as videos? You'll meet some of them and learn when they're sending video in the next chapter. Here in this chapter are characteristics they have in common. If three or four of these six signs resonate with you, it's time to rehumanize your sales process and customer experience with simple webcam and smartphone videos.

SIGN 1: YOU TEACH, TRAIN, SELL, OR SERVE

Anyone working in a professional capacity can benefit from this approach, including you. That's because each of us influences and persuades every day. Best-selling author Daniel Pink takes on this topic in his *New York Times*, *Wall Street Journal*, and *Washington Post* bestseller *To Sell Is Human: The Surprising Truth About Moving Others*. Published at the end of 2012, Pink's book was based on a first-of-its-kind study titled, "What Do You Do at Work?"

Among the top findings from responses of more than 9,000 participants from a range of professions is that, "People are now spending about 40% of their time at work engaged in non-sales selling—persuading, influencing, and convincing others in ways that don't involve anyone making a purchase." We consider non-sales selling crucial to our professional success and know that we should devote more time to it. Of the participants, 37% reported spending significant time teaching, coaching, or instructing people, and 39% spend significant time in service to clients or customers. And a strong majority, 70%, spend significant time persuading or convincing others.[1] Our successes are not exclusively our own; they're shared. We need to work with, for, and through other people to achieve our desired outcomes.

It should come as no surprise, especially after reading Chapter 2, that we spend most of our time in our inboxes. This study found the same to be true. Participants spend more time reading and responding to emails than anything else. Face-to-face conversations and attending meetings were next up. We communicate, connect, and convert most effectively when we're in person, but we spend massive amounts of time mired in text—typing it out, editing it, reading it, interpreting it, replying to clear up misunderstandings, and on. It doesn't have to be this way. Teaching, training, serving, and selling with video conveniently helps bridge the gap between email and face-to-face conversation.

SIGN 2: YOU DRIVE OPPORTUNITIES TOWARD FACE-TO-FACE MEETINGS

By form fill, referral, inbound, outbound, or some other means, an opportunity is created. We reach out with the goal of a reply or response. We often work toward an initial phone call to connect with the person, learn about him or her, do some discovery and diagnosis, and set a face-to-face appointment. For some salespeople, the appointment is in person. For others, it may be by live video conference. For most, the lead follow-up and nurturing process drives toward a form of face-to-face meeting. Why? Because we're better at connecting, influencing, and persuading in person.

This process is common among people who sell software solutions, help buy and sell real estate, sell peace of mind through insurance, manage financial futures, recruit and hire talent, or employ a similar sales process. This might include, for example, a private high school that generates interest online by publishing website pages, blog posts, or downloadable guides about the challenges and opportunities facing today's high school students who are aspiring to gain acceptance to top-tier colleges. Initial contact begins the process of follow-up and discovery. Contact and micro-conversions through videos, emails, text messages, and phone calls ultimately drive to an in-person appointment. The goal of the meeting is to conclude with another scheduled meeting or with the ultimate conversion of a signed contract or another formal commitment that says, "Yes, I choose you and your product or service."

So, why not get face to face earlier and more often? Many professionals use personal videos to generate that initial reply, to confirm before and follow up after appointments, to differentiate themselves from competitors, and to accelerate the sales cycle. Of our customers, 81% report an increase in replies and responses to video emails compared to traditional emails; one in six doubled or more than doubled their reply rate. And 68% report higher lead conversion.

Some businesses and organizations play this exclusively as a numbers game—generating large quantities of online leads, automating the entire follow-up process, and profitably closing 0.9% or 1.4% of those opportunities. You can drop videos into an automated process to help build some personal connection and communicate messages more clearly. But reaching out to someone who's expressed interest in your product or service with a one-to-one video, including a personal subject line and personal video thumbnail or animated preview takes you from, "Yes, I get more replies and responses" to the segment of one in six people who reported a doubling or more than doubling in reply rate with video.

The right answer for you and your team may be a balance of personal and automated, so we cover both throughout this book. Regardless, starting the relationship with a video shows that you work differently, puts your face with your name, allows you to speak directly to each person's interest, and triggers our innate sense of reciprocity. People feel not just an obligation to reply, but also a *need* to reply. And the entire process of driving toward a face-to-face appointment is accelerated. Remember, they'll feel like they know you when you finally connect in real time.

SIGN 3: YOU WANT TO IMPROVE CUSTOMER EXPERIENCE

The success stories we hear from people adding video into their business communication remind us how valuable a personal touch at the right time can be to a business relationship. But they also remind us just how *low* the bar can be for customer experience. A friend of mine runs a residential construction business. He's told me several stories in which his company wins jobs to build new decks, roofs, or siding just by showing up for the appointment. Often, the companies he's competing with don't even show up for their scheduled appointments! It still shocks me that simply honoring your word can be a differentiator.

I've also heard several stories in which sending a video wins the deal against competitors who are sending traditional emails. We're still early enough in this movement that sending a video is remarkable. It's got a surprise-and-delight element to which people respond favorably. As an initial touch, you're setting a tone for how the service will be delivered—whether it's an online class, a software onboarding, a financial plan, a real estate transaction, a home improvement project, or anything else. You're starting to build a relationship digitally. And you're displaying a level of care.

You can add this human touch anywhere in the customer or employee lifecycle. As someone transitions from one status to another with you, the onboarding or training needs can be addressed in part with videos. Make one truly personal and unique to each person and then record the follow-ups once and use them over and over again with other people making the same transition. What are the topics for a series of videos like this? List the frequently asked questions. What do people moving from one stage to another tend to ask at each transition? Answer these questions in videos to save yourself time, to inform and prepare people, to assure smooth and efficient transitions, and to improve the experience.

What happens when someone reaches out with a problem, challenge, question, or fear? Whether positive, negative, or neutral, any inquiry is more quickly, personally, and thoroughly addressed with a video that assesses the situation, draws potential or real paths forward, and recommends one if appropriate. Or you can proactively reach out with an update or progress report, as my friend's team members do from the roof of a client's home to show and tell. Think about that. A crew's on your roof. You're at work. And you get a personal update from your roof. That's service.

One of the most effective videos our customer support team sends to people with a complicated issue is a screen recording from inside that customer's account, walking through potential causes and solutions. The alternative is a mountain of typed-out text and links to support articles that may address the issue. Which is a better experience—a specific video walkthrough inside your account or what looks like a huge homework assignment? Customer satisfaction surveys and time-to-resolution measures strongly favor video.

When a transaction closes or a contract is signed, what's a nice touch to make that can be experienced more than once and shared with others? Send a video thanking the person and noting a highlight or two about the journey. How do you stay in touch with people in a meaningful way so that you're top of mind when they or other people they know are in need of your product or service? Send monthly videos out providing entertaining or informative tips and updates related to you, your business, and your industry. This line of Q&A can go on and on, because a great customer experience is based in timely, relevant, and helpful communication.

Any touch you're making—or *should* be making—to reduce friction and improve customer experience can be done with video. In increasingly digital environments, that human element goes a long way to build trust, allay fears, and avoid pitfalls. If you're not humanizing the experience, then you risk disintermediation.

SIGN 4: YOU RISK DISINTERMEDIATION BY WEB APPS, TOOLS, AND AUTOMATIONS

Two large segments of professionals whose video use we frequently observe are real estate agents and mortgage loan officers. Some real estate professionals fear Zillow. These agents question its business model of selling competitive ads around homes they've listed for sale. They challenge the pricing model or execution of that advertising. They criticize "Zestimated" home values. And they speculate that Zillow may get directly involved in transactions or become a brokerage, something the company consistently refutes. The fear of those agents: that Zillow will eliminate the agent from the transaction—that they'll be disintermediated or cut out of the process.

Many mortgage loan officers feel the same way about Rocket Mortgage from Quicken Loans. Many financial advisors look at Wealthfront or Betterment with skepticism at best and derision at worst. The process is faceless, they observe. Who can you sit down with when things go sideways, they ask. Things go better and people are happier with a real handshake, they say. And for many consumers, these observations are all fair and true. They prefer that human touch and personal service. But for many other consumers, the value and convenience these tools and apps provide makes them highly desirable.

Classic business stories of disruptions, like Blockbuster losing out to streaming services like Netflix, countless booksellers and other retailers folding to Amazon, and taxis with expensive hood medallions tailing Uber and Lyft car services are always at hand and often told. The proverbial "cheese" of the intermediary or "middleman" has already been moved. Or it's currently moving . Or it'll start moving soon. This is disintermediation and all kinds of apps, tools, automations, and services are advancing its march. So, what's a human to do?

The list of jobs being affected is lengthy. An easy go-to here is the driverless car and, even more consequently, the driverless truck. The driver's job is reassigned to the machine; he or she has been disintermediated. Some jobs are being reassigned to the customer herself or himself – and have been for years. Long gone are the days of gas station attendants pumping your gas (unless you're in New Jersey or Oregon). Self-checkout has spread from grocery stores to Target to Home Depot and beyond. To use the language of

Paul R. Daugherty and H. James Wilson in their book *Human+Machine: Reimagining Work in the Age of AI*, the progression is:

- Standardization (Henry Ford, assembly line)
- Automation (1970s–1990s business process reengineering)
- Adaptation (artificial intelligence, big data, and machine learning)

The negative view of all this progress is that it represents cold, cost-reducing approaches with no regard for people, while the positive view is that humans are freed to engage in more varied, stimulating, and productive work environments. The truth will play out somewhere in between.

Your ability to avoid disintermediation by a web app, digital tool, or process automation is in the value you provide. If the value of your contribution to the product or service delivery fails to exceed the cost of the labor you personally provide, you're no longer needed. The value and cost here may be real or simply perceived. But the result will be the same, so you must add value.

Humans win when we employ creativity, expertise, judgment, emotion, social skills, leadership, and other subtleties that are difficult to digitize. We also win when we reply on apps, tools, and automations that remove the monotony, repetition, and heavy lifting that keep us from being our best selves and doing what we do best. In the words of Daugherty and Wilson, "As sales and marketing have become more digital, they have lost some of the personal touch that attracted many to the field in the first place. AI is giving salespeople and marketers the time and insights to cut through the high volume and opacity of digital interactions and letting them be more human."[2]

Review and rehumanize processes that are missing the personal touch. Include personal video and deploy the best web apps, tools, and automations you've got available to help. Disintermediation is driven by customer experience, not by technology itself. You're either adding value to the customer experience or you're just making its delivery more expensive. Don't just hope and expect that people recognize your value; promise it, deliver it, then prove you delivered it. Don't assume that consumers will always prefer to pay to have a human in the process; contribute in such a way that they *want* the human, even at additional cost.

SIGN 5: YOU BENEFIT FROM WORD OF MOUTH

Reaching out. Keeping in touch. Staying top of mind. Along with delivering an excellent customer experience, these are your precursors to positive word of mouth, repeat business, personal referrals, and online reviews. When you, your brand, or your company reminds people who you are, reiterates the value you provide, and continues to provide new value, your name is available when the conversation comes up at the office, in the gym, or around the restaurant table. Do you have an insurance person? A CRM? A financial planner or tax advisor? A preferred video app? Who do you know who can help me make some improvements to my home before putting it on the market? Do you know a person or an app that can help me generate more online leads?

We like to recommend people, products, services, brands, and companies. It feeds our urge to help other people and it taps into our sense of mastery. Is your name the one we provide? Without a referral, a consumer's search for help turns from friends, family, and coworkers to the internet. You may play that game well, but it can be expensive to buy or work your way to the top of the right search results. Ideally, of course, you're in a both/and situation— the great experience you deliver earns word of mouth and you also show up well online.

Keeping in touch and staying top of mind through a consistent stream of personal videos is a great way to earn referrals indirectly. You can also ask for them explicitly from time to time. Some professionals close every video with a hard or soft request for referral. Others use changes in seasons, market conditions, or special offers to present a reason to refer. The best make it easy to refer them by using very specific language about themselves or their contact information. Your clients will adopt your language when you use it with consistency, frequency, and repetition.

Even more than with referrals, the key to winning online reviews is to ask for them. Specifically, the key is asking the right people at the right time. After positive customer interactions, send a video. You can automate them, but they're even better when personal. Thank them. Remind them about the experience and a fun or challenging experience along the way. Position the review as a benefit not just to you, but to other people just like them who deserve the same level of care, service, and support. Provide a link to your preferred review site, along with basic instruction about what awaits after the click. Your ability to link is one of the reasons video email is an ideal medium for this ask. Not only are you more persuasive, you can also send them exactly where they need to go and know exactly who has and *hasn't* yet clicked that link.

But we're already generating great word of mouth without video, you offer. Great! This means you're effective at building trusting relationships, providing real value, and staying top of mind. You're in perfect position to do this at scale using video. If you're already winning these favors from your satisfied clients, it's either just happening as a natural outcome or you're explicitly asking by email or in person. If it's just happening, asking will make it happen a lot more often. If you're asking in person, you're missing scale. If you're asking by text email, you're overestimating your effectiveness. A face-to-face request is 34 times more effective than the same request in a typed-out email, according to a study published recently in the *Journal of Experimental Social Psychology*.[3] That's a dramatic lift!

But we don't like asking favors of our customers and clients, you share. That's fine. We all have a fear of rejection; it's fundamental to the human experience. The vulnerability you'd display in asking for help is attractive, even if it doesn't feel that way. Humility is a good look, especially to people you've served well. If rejection isn't your hang-up and instead it's about the imposition of the ask, here's the resolve. Per a phenomenon dubbed the Ben Franklin Effect, being asked for favors creates liking toward the person making the request. We like doing favors; we form social bonds through this give and take. It triggers a sense of reciprocity, so don't be afraid. Don't hold back. And don't rely on plain text to get the job done.

SIGN 6: YOU WIN MORE OPPORTUNITIES FACE TO FACE

Among these six signs you should be mixing simple videos into your communication flow, this final one is like the first. It's a catch-all. Whether we directly sell or support products and services or we indirectly represent or advance ideas and opportunities, we're more effective face to face. Yes, you can build a real relationship through live video meetings and asynchronous video exchanges, but they're both inferior to being there in person. There's a reason we talk specifically about meeting "IRL" (in real life). It's different. And better.

BombBomb's Chief Marketing Officer and my coauthor, Steve, lives and works outside Philadelphia. Nearly our entire company lives in Colorado Springs and works in our downtown office. Steve schedules one-on-one meetings via Zoom. He joins group meetings the same way. Slack, video email, traditional emails, text messages, and social media help close the gap. But he always takes care to come to the office at least a half dozen times each year, because there's nothing better than face to face. There's a feel to it—a complete understanding, a fuller knowing. When he led a re-engineering of our inside sales process to bolster its consultative nature, he came to Colorado

Springs for a week. The re-engineering took about six weeks, but it would have taken longer and been less effective if he'd not invested in that face time.

But we can't always be there in person. In Steve's case, distance keeps us apart; he simply can't visit the office every day. Do you have employees or customers who are down the street? Across town? Across the state? Throughout the region? Across the country? Around the world? No matter how far through that string of questions you made it with affirmative answers, distance is part of the equation that results in your failure to get together with people as often as you need or want to. Another part of that equation is time. We simply don't have the time to travel to and connect with everyone directly.

You know intuitively that you communicate more clearly, connect more effectively, and convert at a higher rate when you're face to face. But time and distance keep you apart from the people who matter most to your business. The next best thing is video. It overcomes distance in that you can send yourself anywhere in the world nearly instantly. And when that video is asynchronous—recorded and sent when it's convenient for you and opened up and watched when it's convenient for your recipient—it also overcomes time. You don't have to schedule an appointment at a specific time and you don't have to interrupt someone with the expectation of meeting right now. Few communication channels offer both of these benefits *and* get you face to face.

SIX SIGNS THAT YOU NEED PERSONAL VIDEO

Can personal video help you rehumanize your business, accelerate your sales, and improve your customer experience? Should you start replacing some of your typed-out text with webcam or smartphone videos? How many of these signs are true of you and your team?

At least two of the signs recapped in Figure 4.1 are true of everyone— the first and last. And most of the others are true of everyone working in a professional capacity. The fact of the matter is that we've relied too long on faceless digital communication to get important and valuable jobs done. We're over-reliant on a medium that doesn't build trust, doesn't differentiate us, and doesn't communicate as well as looking someone in the eye through the lens and talking to him or her in a personal, casual, and natural way.

So, what does this look like in practice? The next chapter gives you nine specific stories of individuals and teams who are rehumanizing their businesses with personal videos and 10 specific times to use video instead of text.

FIGURE 4.1 Six Signs That You Need Personal Video

1 YOU TEACH, TRAIN, SELL, OR SERVE

2 YOU DRIVE OPPORTUNITIES TOWARD
FACE-TO-FACE MEETINGS

3 YOU WANT TO IMPROVE CUSTOMER EXPERIENCE

4 YOU RISK DISINTERMEDIATION BY WEB
APPS, TOOLS, AND AUTOMATIONS

5 YOU BENEFIT FROM WORD OF MOUTH

6 YOU WIN MORE OPPORTUNITIES
WHEN YOU'RE FACE TO FACE

 **PART**

2

When to **Rehumanize with Video**

CHAPTER 5

Nine Stories of Sales Acceleration and Better Customer Experience

"I consider myself to be in sales in the sense that my students are my customers," says Dr. Daniel Smith, PhD, CRC, NCC, LMHC. An adjunct professor at the University of Buffalo and Canisius College, Dan says that a simple webcam video from his desk "allows me to stand head and shoulders above other teachers because I can reach out and create a relationship with my students." Of course, he shared that with us by sending a personal video, something he's done more than 1,400 times.

Because he's an online professor, Dan teaches counseling and therapy to students across the United States and around the world. He rarely meets any of them in person, so he takes care to communicate face to face in his emails. To start a semester, he sends an introductory video to the entire class. He puts a face with the name and lets the students know with warmth and sincerity that he's available whenever they need him. What a great start to a working relationship.

When a student makes an inquiry at any point during the semester, he promises a reply within 24 hours. Instead of typing out long responses, he clicks "Record" and talks to the student. When he gives feedback on exams, papers, or other significant projects, he doesn't just provide a letter grade, some marks in red pen, and a few margin notes. Dan delivers feedback rich with nonverbal communication to inform and inspire in a way that rewards high performing students and lights a fire under those whose performance needs improvement.

> "That student feels special. That student feels respected. And that student feels like they are part of the class."

As a counselor in high-conflict divorce cases, Dan sends videos to parents, children, and attorneys at times when emotions often run high. Progress starts by building trust and rapport with all the stakeholders in a case. It continues when he takes care to get the tone of the message just right or to empathize with one of the people involved. Not only does video help him do these things more effectively, it also helps him get the same message delivered to everyone at the same time without having to make a series of phone calls.

As an instructor and as a counselor, Dan sees himself as being in the "change" business. Behavior change happens only through human connection and a sense of relationship. Figuring out how to meaningfully connect online was paramount to him and he deemed traditional digital communication insufficient. "It's just as easy for me to send a video as it is to type out an email," says Dan, adding that personal video allows him to "reach into their living room, their study, and create a relationship."

> "The person you're trying to facilitate change in is a human being, not a human doing. Email is *doing*. Video email is the essence of *being*. It is the tool to establish this relationship."

This philosophy and practice are so effective for Dan that he was asked to make a video for tenured professors in the brick and mortar school about how to build relationships through video. What's the measure that earned him this attention? Student feedback at the end of each semester. His customers value his service.

AUTHOR DAN PINK AND PROFESSOR DAN SMITH

When you look back to the opening line of this chapter, Dan Smith sounds a lot like Dan Pink, bestselling author of *Drive: The Surprising Truth About What Motivates Us*; *A Whole New Mind: Why Right-Brainers Will Rule the Future*; and *When: The Scientific Secrets of Perfect Timing*, among other titles. The similarity in the perspective of these Dans comes from Pink's *To Sell Is Human*, also a bestseller.

Like Smith, Pink sees himself as a salesperson. "I am a salesman . . . I spend a significant portion of my days trying to coax others to part with resources."[1] But most of what he does isn't direct selling. His sales activities include:

- Getting an editor to drop a bad story idea
- Getting a business partner to team up
- Getting an organization to change strategy
- Getting a gate agent to assign him an aisle seat
- Getting strangers to read articles he wrote
- Getting friends to do him favors
- Getting his son to take a shower

Nearly everyone operating in professional capacity is challenged with persuading, influencing, and moving others, even when not engaged in direct selling. Access to information grew exponentially because of the internet, so it's no longer asymmetrical. Both sides in most business relationships have approximately equal access to information. This raises the importance of honesty, transparency, and directness.

You can no longer trade on what you know that the other party doesn't. Putting yourself in others' shoes and getting into others' heads is the key to selling yourself, your ideas, your products, and your services. When working with others, don't just make statements, ask questions; this forces people to engage. Don't lean on scripts; few situations are sufficiently stable, predictable, and consistent for them to be effective. Do lean on a higher sense of purpose; this motivates people in a transcendent way. To "combine the efficiency of electronic communication with the intimacy of seeing another person's face and hearing her voice," as Pink writes, send a video.

In this chapter, you'll meet people in a variety of roles who achieve their desired outcomes more quickly and more often by rehumanizing their business processes with video. As you read their stories, think about how the use of video compares with the use of text. Think about similar situations in which you've found yourself and about how personal video might have accelerated your process or improved your outcome.

THE MOST IMPORTANT SOUND IN ANY LANGUAGE

For more than 20 years, Michael Thorne has been helping people buy and sell homes just southeast of Vancouver, British Columbia. Having built a name and reputation in his community, Michael often receives inquiries from prospective clients he's never met. One email from a family thinking about selling their home was signed by all four members—Ryan, Amy, Oliver, and Violet. With thousands of dollars in professional video equipment sitting off his left shoulder in the frame shown in Figure 5.1, Michael held out his iPhone to record and send a video reply.

Why not use the DSLR camera, fancy microphone, and professional lights? Speed and authenticity. Even a semi-formal production process inhibits both. He's sent thousands of simple, mobile videos from varied locations like the airport tarmac, a ferry deck, a car dealership, a conference stage (while presenting), neighborhood streets, and more. To create marketing videos, he uses a Canon 80D, Insta360, GoPro Fusion, DJI drone, and other cameras. "The last camera I'd be willing to give up," says Michael, "is my iPhone." He proudly rocked an iPhone 5S for four years before upgrading to the X.

Expensive equipment and formal production reduce speed and authenticity.

FIGURE 5.1 Quickly Record and Send Mobile Videos

In the video, Michael greeted each of the family members by name before introducing himself, thanking them for their interest, and proposing to meet at their home the next night at 7 p.m. As he prepared for the appointment, Michael noticed that the video was viewed more than a dozen times. Interesting! With more curiosity than trepidation about that, he walked up to their front door a couple of minutes before 7 o'clock and gave it a knock. He heard inside the sound of little feet running up to the front door.

When the front door opened, five-year-old Oliver greeted him: "Michael! Michael! Michael!" Turns out, Oliver was so enamored of being greeted by name, he asked his parents to watch the video over and over before going to bed the previous night. A dozen times. If you're a parent, you know that "Again! Again!" drill when your child's excited about something. The familiarity built through his video not only assured Michael the opportunity to list and sell the home, it also accelerated the formation of trust so well that the family was perfectly comfortable allowing their young child to open the door and welcome into their home a person they'd never met.

When you're recording a truly personal video, take care to say the name of each recipient right off the top to immediately capture full attention and to let each person know the message is specifically for her or him. Author of the classic *How to Win Friends and Influence People*, Dale Carnegie famously reminds us that a person's own name is the sweetest and most important sound that could be spoken. More recently, a study titled, "Brain Activation When Hearing One's Own and Others' Names" found "unique brain functioning activation specific to one's own name in relation to the names of others."[2] The patterns of activation when we hear our own name are similar to those when we make personal judgments, so we're speaking even more to each person when we speak his or her name. Inserting the person's "[first_name]" into the subject line or email body does not have the same effect. While it may "personalize" the message, it doesn't make it truly *personal*.

Visit BombBomb.com/BookBonus to see Michael's video.

As a fun, child-related addition, here's another "that would never have happened with a traditional email reply" story featuring Michael's partner in RE Video Studio, a real estate education project and community. Jesse Peters serves clients in Winnipeg, Manitoba, and uses video in all aspects of his business. One afternoon, Jesse was outside in his yard, where his daughter was blowing bubbles. He received an inquiry from a couple thinking about buying a home.

Comfortable on camera anywhere, Jesse started recording a quick video reply thanking the person for her interest and promising a phone call when he got inside. No matter that he was wearing a ballcap. No matter that the breeze cut wind noise across his phone's mic. And no matter that he was interrupted while recording. During his first and only take, his darling daughter toddled over to the camera, waved, and said, "Hi" before walking back out of the shot to blow more bubbles. Rather than stop and re-record the video because of this interruption, Jesse just sent it as-is, which he does for every one of his personal videos.

Not only did Jesse land the appointment, the couple brought a bubble bottle and wand for his daughter. He's enjoyed many other beautifully human experiences as a consequence of videos sent before and after every appointment. He wins against competitors because of it, too. You don't need a "perfect" video to build relationships and win opportunities.

LEADERSHIP, VIDEO, AND THE HANDWRITTEN NOTE

Based in Louisville, Kentucky and serving as regional President and CEO of four different companies, Brad DeVries leads more than 1,300 people spread across multiple offices in multiple cities. If you lead remote workers or large teams and find it important to lead with a personal touch, adopt his practice. Just four years into his use of personal videos, Brad's recorded and sent more than 5,000. Most are one-to-one, but he also uses video for all-company messages.

For happy birthdays, holiday greetings, thank-yous, milestone celebrations, company-wide announcements, and even more significant moments, such as deaths in the family, Brad looks people in the eye through video. Writing slows him down and limits his ability to express gratitude, excitement, or sympathy. Using video to build relationships is a "no brainer," in his words. He adds that "If I could only keep one personal tool to be able to reach out to everybody," it would be video messages.

Similar to Brad, Todd Bland serves more people in more stakeholder groups than he can regularly see in person. As Head of School at the Milton Academy, a K–12 college preparatory school just south of Boston, Todd takes a personal, authentic approach to leadership. Parents and students, faculty and staff, alumni and donors—they all deserve a high level of attention and care. Congratulations. Happy birthday. Thank you for your generous gift. These messages are better delivered in video than in typed or handwritten words. "Having to write a lot of thank-you notes and expressing appreciation for good work—I love doing that, but being able to do that in my own voice" allows Todd to add humor, personality, and authenticity.

Like email, the handwritten note can't be replaced. Given the huge swing toward digital and automated messages, its stock is up these days. We'll bypass the robotic, automated handwriting services designed to make people think you actually took the time to write it yourself (don't get me started) and observe two specific benefits of a truly handwritten note:

1. I made this just for you. I cared enough to spend the time.
2. My personality is on the page. Through my handwriting, I'm expressing thoughts and feelings in a way that's completely unique to me.

A one-to-one video message does both of these things—and arguably does them better. When you greet someone by name and speak specifically about her or his birthday, milestone, or hardship, it's obvious you did so just for that person. A reply like "thank you so much for taking the time to make that video for me" comes often, even though clicking "Record" and talking is almost always faster than typing or writing the same message. And when you send a video message, you're sending yourself. You're not one in a million—you're one of a kind. Whether it's big, bold, and boisterous or mellow, subdued, and measured, your unique personality makes your video one that only you can send.

Don't let the simplicity of this activity fool you into thinking it's not effective. You don't have to complicate your use of video for it to pay off significantly. Don't have fancy video equipment? Neither do Brad or Todd. Don't know when to use video? Send on the occasions they do. Afraid of being on camera? These are people who already know and like you. Maya Angelou famously observed that "people will forget what you said, people will forget what you did, but people will never forget how you made them feel." It feels great to be noticed. Showing that you notice shows that you care. Caring connects us.

APPRECIATION YOU CAN FEEL

The people at Care and Share Food Bank for Southern Colorado believe no one should go hungry, so they distribute more than 20 million pounds of food every year through nearly 300 partner agencies to feed people in more than 30 counties. To serve the mission, they rely on employees, volunteers, corporate financial and food donors, individual donors, partner agencies, governments and government agencies, foundations and grants, the Feeding America organization and network, and people in other stakeholder groups.

As part of their strategic planning, leadership hosts "listening sessions" with these stakeholder groups to learn how to serve each of them more effectively and create more win-win situations. I attended one for corporate donors who give time or money to support the food bank's mission. "You all are so good with those videos," said one of the attendees. "We love them and forward them around the company every time." This is something Project Manager and long-time Chief Operating Officer Stacy Poore noticed in their video email analytics. "You can see that more than just the recipient is opening and viewing, and sometimes the recipient is viewing multiple times."

So, what are they sending? Something you can send every day: sincere gratitude. Simple thank-you videos like the one in Figure 5.2. Together, Stacy, CEO Lynne Telford, Chief Alliance Officer Shannon Brice, Individual Giving Director Becky Treece, Community Engagement Director Eric Pizana, and other team members have sent nearly 2,000 personal videos in just a couple of years. "We use them in many ways—to connect with volunteers, thank donors, make fun announcements, and more. I'm really glad we have the tool and I think it differentiates us from other nonprofits, which is very important!" says Stacy, adding, "One of the things I've realized more with this tool than ever before, and I knew this already, is that people are not thanked nearly often enough."

Whether in direct sales or in nonprofit work, "thank you" goes a long way. Expressing gratitude is like smiling, which provides physical and

FIGURE 5.2 A "Thank-You" Video Delivers Appreciation You Can Feel

psychological benefits for both its wearer and its viewer. A deep body of research supports the idea that saying thank you alerts the recipient of potential for a high-quality social bond. In a study titled, "Warm Thanks: Gratitude Expression Facilitates Social Affiliation in New Relationships via Perceived Warm," researchers found that expressions of appreciation increased the likelihood that a "novel peer" (someone you've never met) provides contact information for follow up and "prompted investment in the burgeoning social bond."[3] It doesn't just maintain and advance relationships, appreciation helps establish them.

Seeing "Thanks" or "Thank you" in typed-out text is like seeing your name. It's so ubiquitous it's nearly meaningless. Just as marketing automation inserts our names and other details into subject lines and email bodies, we drop in these words and phrases without much thought or effort. What's personalized with automation is not necessarily personal. And we can feel the difference.

When you look people in the eye, greet them by name, and use the full range of human expression to let him or her know how appreciative you are, it comes to life. That's why an organization like Care and Share, with an annual budget of nearly $50 million, reaches out in one-to-one messages to people engaged in their fight against hunger.

MORE SALES REPLIES AND FEWER SUPPORT REPLIES

A technology service company with more than 7,000 global employees recognized the power of personal video and engaged us to implement it. Mapping video opportunities to their desired outcomes, our Enterprise Solutions Director James Stites put together pilot studies with their inside sales and client success teams. The former sought an increase in replies from customers who were using their service at no cost to talk about paid upgrades. The latter sought a decrease in replies and an increase in customer satisfaction as they resolved inquiries and issues related to their services.

Both teams were equipped with our tool set to record and send personal videos and screen recordings from directly inside their Gmail inboxes. Neither team had video assigned as a required performance metric; it was a secondary system to their primary platform. Our team dashboard shows open and reply rates on every Gmail send, plus play rates when those sends included videos. Managers could see this by individual and across the team.

The 40 salespeople in the pilot sent more than 800 videos in a 55-day period, an average of 21 videos per person. Most included a whiteboard with the recipient's name written on it, a smile, a personal greeting, a message about how they can improve their recruiting and hiring with paid services, and a request to respond to learn more. The reply rate for first-touch sends to relatively cold opportunities was 55.6% higher with video than without (9.8% versus 6.3%). Among those who played the video, the reply rate jumped to 21.9%. And on follow-up sends, video emails generated a 12.8% higher reply rate than traditional emails. Open rates on video sends were higher in both cases, too.

We were also able to give them specific insights to continue improving those results. For example, sends on Tuesdays, Wednesdays, and Thursdays produced 80% of the replies and had the highest likelihood of receiving a reply within 24 hours. Sends before 8 a.m. and after 5 p.m. had the highest open rates at 89.3% and 84.5%, respectively. In contrast, sends between 8 a.m. and 5 p.m. were opened at a rate 10 percentage points lower (ranging from 69.5% to 73.1%). These findings are consistent with the always-on nature of email we explained in Chapter 2.

For better prospecting, send personal videos to introduce yourself and the opportunity. Send some mid-week outside normal office hours.

The customer success team engaged 30 members for their pilot. To resolve issues, answer questions, and improve customer experience, they sent 688 total videos during the study—an average of 22.9 videos per person. Video and non-video sends had open rates greater than 70% but replies to the video sends were 33% lower (6.0% versus 8.9%). While your sales team seeks engagement and response, your customer success team seeks resolution and satisfaction as quickly as possible. A decrease in customer replies is an *increase* in efficiency.

So, responding to customers by talking rather than typing improves efficiency. But what about satisfaction? Of the customers, 85.37% rated the video sends as "very helpful" or "extremely helpful." And the verbatim feedback explains why. People who filled out the post-service survey commented on the quality of communication, the personal nature of video, and even a love of the practice. Among their responses about the simple webcam videos sent from Gmail:

> "At a time of automated attendants or robots, or even chats, it's good to see a real person even if it's just a recording. This is a great customer service idea!"
> "The video made the service feel more personal, and I thought it was nice that I could see who I was talking to on the phone-thank you (employee name)! It feels like the customer service really cared and looked into our situation."
> "More personal than a voicemail or email."
> "(Employee name) rocks! I love the video and was shocked that it was personalized!"
> "I LOVED this format of reply—so personalized! Thank you!"
> "Polite voicemail was left, but the emailed video was novel, engaging, and impressive! Well done, thanks!"

Better than a bot. Seeing *and* feeling. Connecting with and naming a specific person. Moving people from confused or frustrated to satisfied and pleased. All this is as simple as clicking "Record" and talking to a customer conversationally, as if you're sitting across the table from her or him. The common denominator in increasing replies to prospecting emails and increasing efficiency in service, support, and success is the same: rehumanizing the process with simple videos.

EVEN MORE SUCCESS IN CUSTOMER SUCCESS

An 81.9% decrease in time-to-resolution, 55.2% and 13.8% increases in one-touch resolution with evergreen videos and personal videos, respectively, and a 40.9% increase in satisfaction survey response rate (31% versus 22%) with nearly equal satisfaction rates (98% versus 97%). These are the early results of our own Customer Success team using BombBomb videos inside Zendesk, the leading cloud-based customer service software (see Figure 5.3). Just over 15,000 tickets into organizing the data more clearly through this integration, the benefits of video are clearer than ever.

Just as we have for sales, marketing, and other functions, our team's been using video for customer success for years. But now, with the Zendesk integration, it's more directly aligned with our care associates' day-to-day workflow and provides better insights into video's efficacy. As any support professional will tell you, you're often interacting with people when they're confused or frustrated at best and upset or angry at worst. As a result, "we spend a lot of time in support trying to get the right tone," says Donovan Steinberg, Director of Customer Success. People often make up their minds in advance about what their experience is going to be, so a helpful and specific video message can make a huge impact by exceeding those expectations. It's easy to feel like you're just another number, another ticket, or another phone call, so a personal video breaks that pattern.

Which videos do they record once and use over and over? They've produced a couple dozen "evergreen" videos with product or feature walkthroughs and known-issue workarounds to address the most common questions. "These are vital for scaling," says Paul Case, Customer Care Manager. Beyond direct service, they use evergreen videos to improve the service experience. "Thank you for your feature request" and "Thank you for your time on the phone today" are examples of videos ideal for prerecording and adding to a workflow automation. Any interaction that happens often and with little variation is a prime candidate.

Which videos do they make truly personal? For any problem or question with multiple potential fixes, a video recorded inside the customer's account

FIGURE 5.3 Improvements for Customer Success

Early Results: Customer Success Video In Zendesk

	NO VIDEO	VIDEO	IMPROVEMENT
Time to Resolution	61 min	11 min	81.9%
First-Touch Resolution Rate	58%	90%	55.1% Evergreen
	58%	66%	13.8% Personal
Survey Response Rate	22%	31%	40.9%
Customer satisfaction	97%	98%	1%

with the screen recorder is far superior to a long, drawn-out email with links to multiple support articles. The former shows you're listening, that you care, and that you're available to diagnose further. The latter feels like work for a frustrated or confused customer. And they have that video to play over and over as needed. The video serves as documentation.

That video replay ability isn't just a win for customers, though. When a ticket gets reopened by another team member, watching the video is a great time-saver compared to reading a long back-and-forth email exchange. Remember the 81.9% decrease in resolution time? It's 11 minutes for video and 61 minutes for typed-out text. Getting the tone right on the first send takes time. And because it's typed-out text, it's not as rich and helpful a piece of communication, so you wind up in an email exchange that takes even more time. One of the reasons video's so quick is due to its ability to produce one touch resolution.

Another great use of a truly personal video is follow-up after a phone call to thank a customer, reiterate the key points, and provide encouragement going forward. Especially because we're helping people build and establish the new habit of getting face to face in simple videos, that follow-up can make a big difference for someone who's short on the clarity or confidence needed to go forward. That type of attention and care doesn't just boost experience and build success, it also breeds loyalty.

Do customers like video? Though their overall satisfaction is only one percentage point higher, people who receive support videos give feedback far more often. Based on what we just shared about evergreen videos and personal videos, can you tell which customers received which style of video from their comments? Also watch for the enthusiastic use of exclamation points, all caps, and first names.

"Thank you so much! Best part was you just sent me the video! That's exactly what I needed! Thanks again!"

"Zach is awesome! He walked me through how to correct the issue I was having via video, which was so helpful. He is VERY knowledgeable!"

"Excellent. Answered all my questions and immediately prepared and sent me a how-to video."

"Excellent—especially when he sent a video to remind me how to use the video to reach customers better."

"Above and beyond. Hands down, THE BEST customer service of any company. Never a long hold, the Customer Service rep is thorough, and I LOVE that you use your own product and put a face with the name by emailing a video after the call. Rea was super encouraging and took it a step further by challenging me to reply to her email with a video and not to watch it after and re-record! And I did it! Lol! Thank you again for your GREAT support!"

Video's benefits are conferred to your team members and to your customers. When you serve customers with empathy and respect instead of treating them like numbers, tickets, and problems, it's rehumanizing for everyone. And video does this better than text. "That's made the difference," observes Paul. "That's why the responses are higher."

THE FIRST SALESPERSON TO SEND 10,000 VIDEOS

"Video helps you establish a relationship in a way you just can't reach with a phone call or text-based email," according to Danny Doerksen, who is likely the first person to record and send 10,000 videos for the purpose of building relationships and increasing revenue. He hit that number in January 2018, about three and a half years into his video journey. As this chapter's being written, Danny's well over 13,000 videos and counting, making him a not-so-average software salesperson. He started as an inside sales representative following up with, nurturing, and converting marketing-generated opportunities. Today, Danny's an enterprise account executive reaching out to C-level and VP-level executives representing large sales teams and entire companies.

Like so many of us, Danny was initially uncomfortable on camera. Out on the sales floor, he was surrounded by a couple dozen people, so he felt self-conscious. But, "You get over it as you send more and more" videos. You can waste two hours sending a 20-second video by rerecording and trying to be perfect. Instead, he recommends that you stop scrutinizing yourself and your videos. "Know that every imperfection adds to the human quality of the message," explains Danny.

Here are a handful of lessons learned on his journey to 10,000 videos and beyond:

- A video play "shows true engagement." Most systems will show you an email open, but you can't tell if a person actually read your message. When someone clicks play, you know they've met you and you can see how long they watched.

- Pair videos with phone calls. "By sending a video email first with my phone number below, I introduce myself and let you know I'm going to give you a call 'at the number below,' " explains Danny, who calls from that now-familiar number shortly after his video gets played.
- If the video *doesn't* get played, "You can't give up." He continues with phone calls, text-based emails, and video emails to produce meaningful engagement. "Video just allows you to diversify your outbounding."
- Always write the person's name or an important, personal detail on a whiteboard or note and hold it up to start the video. This lets each person know that video is specifically for him or her, not a generic, mass send. The result is higher play rates and reply rates.
- Don't type much additional information into the email body; only type in information that drives the video play or reinforces your call to action. "The less text I give them around that video, the more reason they have to push play on it." Text he includes in every send: multiple ways to contact him in his email signature.
- "Don't overthink it any more than you overthink a voicemail." And once you've established some rapport, feel free to have a little fun with it. "I love reaching that point where I can send a goofy video to someone. When you can laugh together with someone, that's when you level up the relationship. As a salesperson, that's exactly where you want to be."

When Danny's in the office, he sends about 20 videos per day. Like you, he talks faster than he types, so it saves him time while also building rapport – a win-win. He tries to keep each video under 45 seconds. The reason he keeps going? "There's no single *aha* moment. You see the relationship you can build so much more quickly with a video. That's what keeps me using it."

A SALES TEAM THAT'S SENT 10,000 VIDEOS

Screen recordings, customer education, rate updates, next steps, lead responses, client check-ins, congratulations, birthdays—Clifton Saunders and his team send all kinds of video emails and video text messages. Together, the four team members drove Amcap Home Loans in Laporte, Texas, past the 10,000-video milestone in just two and a half years. Video's been "a huge game changer" and a time saver for them.

"When it comes to converting leads, introductions to new real estate agents, follow-ups to people I just met, past clients, everyone—video's made all the difference," according to Clifton. In addition to sending simple videos by email, he also takes video links and sends them by text message in this B2C sales process. In both cases, "it goes over very well. I get lots of responses. And they're surprised almost every time. They love it."

Were you the best writer in school, a master of spelling and grammar? Neither was my coauthor Steve. But Steve, like Clifton, shines when he's face to face. Do you write or type quickly? Clifton doesn't, so he used to use Dragon's "talk to text" software to dictate his emails. Now, he just clicks "Record," talks into the camera, then sends the video. He benefits from the time and energy saved by simply speaking as before. But video gives him the added benefit of "showing people I'm a real person" and overcomes the problem that "tone doesn't come through in text messages or emails."

How did he get his team on board with video? He's still working on it but reinforces two main behaviors: come prepared to be on camera and don't think about it too much. While seemingly at odds, these ideas are complementary. Being prepared is not about having a perfect appearance. How you look on camera is how you look in person. If someone doesn't want to work with Clifton or one of his team members due to physical appearance, he feels the same way about that person. Instead, preparation is about mindset. It's about getting out of your own head and out of your own way. "We like to have fun in our videos," says Clifton. "Just be yourself. You'll see instant results as soon as that happens."

Another team with high usage and great results is led by Justen Martin, who gets his team on board with video by recruiting, hiring, and onboarding into a "video-first culture." Five of his iHomes Colorado team members have each sent more than 1,000 videos. A dozen have sent 500 or more, and 50 of them have each sent at least 100 videos. And they've got fewer than 100 active accounts at the time of this tally! They set up a private Facebook group in which team members can practice video recording and get feedback from their peers. Their people and processes are video-oriented because the single most important aspect of their business is how they make clients *feel*. Justen credits their collective, cultural commitment to video with "helping us with our response rates and conversion rates and, more importantly, our service and review rates."

PERSONAL TOUCH, FASTER CONVERSION, AND MORE REFERRALS

"In our industry, as in any sales industry, you want to have as many touches as you can with your potential clients. Before they come in for a visit, after they come in for a visit, and after they become a client," says David Blackston, a financial planner in The Villages, Florida who's sent nearly 1,000 videos in about two years. His team members have sent about 1,000 more. "We never send a video that's specific to anything related to products," explains David. "We use it as a relationship-builder, not as a selling tool." If you're in a business that works to increase appointments set and appointments held, David's processes are for you.

His office sends mass video emails to their entire database regularly, including invitations to client appreciation events like shopping trips and golf outings. Even more valuable, though, are their weekly market update videos. Again, it's never product-focused; they talk about the economy and the markets in general. When the stock market took a negative turn one week, David says that market update video reduced inbound calls dramatically, saving him and his advisors valuable time. Prior to starting that process, they would have taken 50 to 100 inbound calls from nervous, anxious, or curious clients. Now, their clients know what's going on and feel the team's warmth and competence.

More valuable, though, is their process for one-to-one video for prospective clients. As soon as the first visit gets scheduled, he sends a video with a welcome message to convey excitement about having them in and to remind them what to bring to the visit. When they arrive, "it's 100% different" from the way meetings started before he used video. It takes away the anonymity of the financial planner and makes the client feel special. Before the client ever gets home from the initial visit, another personal video from David waits in his or her inbox. He thanks the person for coming in, expresses enjoyment of their time together, previews what they'll do in the next visit, and makes himself available for any questions in the meantime.

One Thursday afternoon, a husband and wife came in for an initial visit with David. As soon as the visit concluded, he recorded and sent a thank-you video. That Friday evening, David's phone lit up with real-time alerts over and over as his video was played 10 times within a half hour. When the couple returned for their second visit, David asked about it. "I loved the video," the husband said. "We were having a dinner party at our house and I was showing all the people how my new advisor communicates." Mind you, David wasn't their "new advisor" on paper, but he was in the hearts and minds of this couple. And they were already referring him to family and friends!

David's team used to get 250 to 275 referrals each year, but since they started sending personal videos and mass video emails, it's been "steadily climbing." And he finds it so easy to do: Recording videos "is like walking down the street." David's tips for you:

- Just get started and do it.
- Smile and wave to start your videos.
- Place the camera above eye level so it's looking down at you rather than up your nose.
- Make sure your background is clean but personal (think: photos of your family).
- Put the majority of your information in the video rather than in the email body.

IT'S NOT ABOUT THE VIDEO

Through these stories, examples, and lessons, you may have started to see where video can fit into your processes. In every case, it's not about the video. Instead, it's about people and relationships. Video is simply a container for your message, just as the words written then printed onto this page are one of the containers we use to convey this philosophy of rehumanizing your business with video. Even if you're not directly selling products or services, you're moving hearts and minds. You're changing people. And video gives you a more personal and powerful way to do it. If you enjoyed some of the tips these practitioners provided, you'll be pleased to know that there are many more in the pages ahead.

CHAPTER 6

———

Ten Times to Use Video Instead of Plain, Typed-Out Text

We know what you're thinking: I'm not going to send a video every time I need to reach out to someone. You're right. You're not. Video isn't always the best answer. Very often, the typed-out messages you've been relying on for years remain the right choice. So when do you go to the "Record" button and when do you go to the keyboard?

We break that down in this chapter with 10 specific situations that are ideal go-to times for video. These are the trigger points or moments when you'll remind yourself, "I should send a video for this." And because video's not always the best choice, you'll also learn when *not* to send a video.

TOP 10 TIMES VIDEO SAYS IT BETTER

For improved clarity, stronger connection, and better results, you need to lead with your face, voice, personality, and expertise from time to time. Speaking your message can say it better than writing it out. Here are 10 specific times this is especially true. You probably experience a few of them every day.

Time 1: Cold Prospecting, First Introduction

Problem: Overcoming the volume of emails that yours competes with, standing out in the inbox, making an impression, generating a reply
Why Video: To let each person know that it's a truly personal touch, to differentiate yourself, to create a remarkable experience, to increase reply rate

It's so easy to delete an email—just a swipe or a click. It's much harder for a person to reject a smiling face than to delete more plain text. So, put a face to your name. Bring your message to life. Reach out in a more personal way earlier in the sales cycle. Say thank you or provide a compliment to enhance the social bond. Offer a link to related information. Track behavior to judge the person's level of interest.

You have two video options here. The first is a canned or evergreen video that's automatically sent over and over as someone fills out a form or otherwise enters your CRM. The second is a true one-to-one video in which you include the person's name or other specific details in the animated preview and right off the top as you start speaking. The latter is obviously more effective, but the former scales better.

Software salesperson Shane Ryan has sent more than 6,000 videos in three years. Most of them are personal sends, each to a specific person. When he's prospecting, he does a few minutes of research on each recipient. Enough to find them on LinkedIn, to identify something they're personally passionate about, to understand what their role and company are responsible for, and to put those together into a must-open, must-play video email.

In the three-second animated preview of his videos, Shane's got a whiteboard message related to the person's passion. Via the screen recorder, he also includes a highly relevant web page, like her or his LinkedIn profile. You can see what that looks like in Figure 6.1. He's refined this technique over time and it's producing more replies and warmer conversations. He's standing out in the inbox and getting results.

If your volume is too high or price point is too low to justify all custom sends, create one or more automated, evergreen videos. Make each as specific to the lead sources as possible. Less "thank you for your interest in (our product or service category)" and more "thank you for requesting a quote on (specific product or service)" or "thank you for downloading our guide to the three best ways to (achieve outcome related to your specific product or service)."

FIGURE 6.1 Let People Know It's Truly Personal

In both cases and if your system provides them, use email open, video play, and link click alerts to know which prospects are most interested and when to follow up. If someone's watching your video right now, she or he is almost certainly available to be reached by phone. Based on others' success with this tactic, refer to your video email in any voicemails you send and refer to your voicemail in any video emails you send. Again, you're putting a face with the name and building trust in order to generate a reply or response.

Time 2: Nurturing Responsive and Unresponsive Leads

Problem: Not getting a clear "yes" or "no," leaving opportunities open, losing ROI by failing to engage open opportunities

Why Video: To start building "know, like, and trust" before you ever meet or even talk on the phone, to differentiate yourself from competitors, to generate replies through reciprocity and social obligation

The sales opportunities that move quickly do so because they get to "yes" or "no" quickly. And then there are the rest. Maybe. Maybe later. Maybe if. Some people say it explicitly and others say it with silence. How do you engage these people? How do you get them off the fence and into action? Adding video to your nurturing process gets you face to face earlier and more often, makes you more persuasive, and helps you judge each person's interest based on their real behavior. Opens, clicks, plays, and replies let you know who to continue following up with and who to let go.

Block time in your day to run through your open opportunities—those responsive and unresponsive leads you've not yet converted or disqualified.

Check in with each person, either by automating or by getting truly personal. We recommend the latter for all responsive lead follow-up. These are people who've replied or taken your call but have stalled out in the path forward. Speak specifically to your prior correspondence, inquire about their status or interest in going forward, and make clear the next step.

For the unresponsive people who've never replied or engaged with you directly, you can get away with more automation, even though personal is better. If you opt to use an evergreen video, be sure to create a few distinct versions— one for each of your most common lead sources or situations. This allows you to provide enough detail or context that it can feel personal. Add any other specifics you can to increase that feeling. For example: "It's been two weeks since you . . ." or "A couple days ago, I left a voicemail . . ." The more specificity an evergreen video has, the more effective it will be.

Time 3: Great to Meet You

> **Problem:** Not standing out or making an impression, failing to capitalize on social interactions like networking events and mutual introductions
>
> **Why Video:** To put your face back together with your name, to create a remarkable experience, to provide all your contact information

After a networking event, conference, or trade show, you've collected a stack of business cards or digital connections. And so has everyone else who attended. Bring your business card to life, stand out from everyone else, and capitalize on the connection by sending a personal video to each person you met. Mention something you had in common, a topic from your conversation, a personal detail you picked up, or an opportunity to pursue. Write a little note on each business card as you collect them to give yourself something to talk about later in the video.

A "great to meet you" video is also useful for unplanned, in-person encounters through a mutual connection. For example, if you're having lunch with a friend or colleague and someone she or he knows comes by to say hello, you'll typically get introduced. If it makes sense and if there's opportunity there, take care to send a video within 24 hours. This gesture lets the person know that it was a meaningful connection.

Your video is often received as a gift of your time and attention, even when it takes no time at all! You can send 10 short, personal videos to send along with your contact information in 15 to 20 minutes. Provide a clear call to action. Do you want to set an appointment, have a brief phone call, connect on social media, or simply deliver your contact information? Was there something specific to move forward that you talked about upon meeting? Or an unanswered question? Keep the conversation going by picking back up in a personal video.

Time 4: Project or Process Update

Problem: Not getting everyone on the same page, allowing information gaps that details fall through, degrading customer experience, slowing progress, or introducing errors through miscommunication

Why Video: To show and tell, to provide "in person" updates that are convenient for everyone, to save time by updating everyone at once, to know who got the update and who didn't

Whether you're working with one person or a team of people, communication is key. But you don't want to type it all out and you can't afford to call each stakeholder about each change or update along the way. Save time by talking in a video instead of typing out multiple paragraphs or calling each person individually. Make complicated, detailed, and nuanced information easier to convey. If there's something that's best explained by showing it, make a screen recording, but be sure to include your face, not just the document, web page, or chart you want to show. By combining face, voice, and visual information, you're supporting a wider range of learning styles. As a courtesy, type out a list of steps or details to go with your video for easy reference so your recipients don't have to pull those notes out of your video themselves.

Because you're recording and sending on your time and each person is opening and playing on his or her own time, you don't have to schedule as many face-to-face appointments. Tracking, analytics, and alerts tell you who's seen it and who hasn't, so you can follow up with people as necessary.

Ruby Grynberg with Salmon Bay Community Lending in Seattle, Washington developed a weekly habit of sending one video to all parties involved in a live mortgage transaction. She and her team brainstormed ways to save time, increase efficiency, and improve customer experience while tackling the most common question they get during the loan process: "What's going on?"

Her team observed that people often have selective hearing and occasionally miss deadlines. They struggled with the fact that "telling one person something doesn't mean that everyone else in the transaction has that information." As captured in Figure 6.2, Ruby stands at an oversized calendar of the next four weeks, marks important events with sticky notes, and explains the next steps in the transaction. She records and sends an update every Friday throughout the process.

Her video is always two minutes or less and starts with a little chalkboard with the buyer's and seller's names on it. It's sent to the two parties and their agents, as well as any other professionals involved in the transaction. This practice has been so effective that they've extended it to other situations. When a purchase offer is written by a buyer they've approved for a loan, they send a similar video to the sellers and the sellers' agent. The quality and timeliness of communication produces a surge in confidence; the sellers know that Ruby and her team are on top of the situation. This gets her buyers' offers accepted more often, especially in competitive situations. Like consumers, business professionals prefer to work with people they know, like, and trust, so this video technique serves her and her clients well. It also humanizes the process.

FIGURE 6.2 Keep Everyone Informed and Prepared throughout the Process

To hear Ruby describe her update process, visit BombBomb.com/BookBonus

From the start of a project or process through the finish, more communication is better than less. It improves customer experience, assures desired outcomes, and creates personal referrals, online reviews, and positive word of mouth.

Time 5: Holidays and Special Occasions

Problem: Sending the same cards or typing the same social posts as everyone else, failing to draw on the emotion inherent in the occasion
Why Video: To look people in the eye and communicate with clarity and emotion, to provide a remarkable experience, to let people know you really care by taking time out of your day

Especially in sales roles, we're always looking for timely and relevant reasons to reach out to people. Fortunately, the calendar is packed with them in the form of holidays and special occasions. On meaningful days in people's lives, send personal videos. On holidays, send one-to-one, one-to-many, or even one-to-all videos. Use fun days related to you or your brand, like International Picnic Day, National Book Lovers Day, or National Guacamole Day as a reason to reach out.

Sure, you can record a single happy birthday video and use it over and over, but it's quick, easy, and fun to make them truly personal. Block time and batch this effort for efficiency. Make a week's or month's worth of video emails in one sitting but use scheduled sending to have each go out on the correct day.

Mark and Laura Anderson, a husband and wife real estate team in Vadnais Heights, Minnesota, have sent more than 2,400 videos, including hundreds of birthday videos. Before one recording, Mark said something Laura found hilarious, so they smiled and laughed through the entire birthday video. Here's the client's reply:

"Thank you both so much for the fun Happy Birthday video!! You both were having such a good time, you made me laugh, too!!
HOPE YOU BOTH HAD WONDERFUL HOLIDAYS AND ARE DOING WELL. Fun to see you in the video:-)
Blessings to you both!!!!!!!"

Have you ever received a response like this to a Facebook or LinkedIn birthday greeting you typed up? Of course not. Not even close. In case you missed it, here's the tally: 11 exclamation points, one line in ALL CAPS, and a smiley face. What was the client trying to do with that expressive text? Give back the thought, care, and positive energy that the Andersons sent her in video. You simply can't create that connective experience for a client with plain text or even a card.

Social media is especially useful here, but not just for messaging. Your social feeds inform you of birthdays and other special occasions. Someone's son got accepted to a desired college? Someone's daughter made captain of the team? Someone landed a new job or achieved a specific success at work? Let people know you're paying attention and that you care with a personal video.

On major holidays, mortgage loan officer Joe Soto from Cypress, California, sends videos to all the people in his database. Even though they're one-to-all sends, he makes them more personal by including his family. When he's joined in videos by his wife, his kids, or their dog, engagement is "super high" compared to other sends. This humanizes Joe and enhances connection to him. In his words: "What I felt was that it puts things on a more personal level. Everybody gets those generic emails on Christmas and Thanksgiving, but very few people show pictures of their family and even fewer have their people speaking with them. It's a great way to connect on a much deeper level."

If you're sending holiday or special occasion emails or cards right now, are you just checking the box? Are you expecting or receiving replies from grateful customers? If your goal is to connect and start conversations, not just check the box, start making a habit of sending five or 10 personal videos each morning for specific occasions or in the lead up to a major holiday. By doing this, you'll stand out from the 50 other emails each person gets on days closer to the actual date of the holiday. In addition, it gives you time to respond to the replies you'll be receiving by spreading out the sends. Don't just check the box. Take full advantage of timely reasons to reach out with video.

Time 6: Bad News or Apology

Problem: Not communicating with enough empathy or clarity, allowing people to read your messages with too much or not enough emotional charge, being misunderstood

Why Video: To convey empathy and sincerity, to communicate your message with the appropriate tone, to provide your viewer the space to process the message

We've all seen the "sorry/not sorry" apology in a press conference of a politician, celebrity, or athlete. We know sincerity and insincerity when we see them. We know when a message is heartfelt and when it's empty and self-serving. We feel it. But a typed-out apology? It's up to the reader. It's easy to be misread or misunderstood. Our intention or meaning can be misconstrued. The written word doesn't capture empathy or care like eye-to-eye, face-to-face communication does. When you leave the door open even an inch to judgments of sincerity, you've given away all control. So, if you need to apologize or share bad news, consider sending a video. But only if you're sincere, because people can see through you otherwise.

Being honest and direct is a winning play. Take for example Mike Minervini's $45,000 apology video. A real estate coach and a former agent from New Jersey, Mike was in Las Vegas attending the international RE/MAX conference when he realized a misunderstanding had occurred with potential clients. They were scheduled to meet the following week, but the couple thought the meeting was the current week, when Mike was out of town. To respond to an angry, confused, and urgent couple, Mike got out his mobile phone in the hotel lobby, recorded an apology, and kindly requested that the meeting be held as scheduled the following week.

In his 30-second video, Mike . . .

- Acknowledged the miscommunication
- Apologized twice
- Confirmed the correct day and time
- Promised specific value in the upcoming appointment
- Closed with a smile

Visit BombBomb.com/BookBonus to see Mike's apology video.

Because of the video, the couple agreed to the meeting and to have Mike list their home for sale. His team also brought the buyer to that transaction and helped them purchase a newly constructed home. Total commission: $45,000. And the couple specifically told him the video message from Las Vegas saved the entire opportunity. We all make mistakes. Owning up to them in a human way is the first step toward making them right.

Beyond miscommunication, misstatements, human errors, and other mistakes that require an apology, you have to break bad news from time to time. Asynchronous video is a helpful medium for this for two reasons: bad news is more psychologically compelling to the recipient and bad news takes longer to cognitively process.[1] When you directly confront someone with bad news on a phone call or in person, the situation demands an immediate response. When you send it in a video recording, you're giving people the time they need to process it. Your ability to manage the tone is improved. Tracking lets you know the message got through, so you can follow up after giving them time to process the news.

"Video isn't the 'secret sauce' recipe" to success according to Nancy Chapin, a sales professional from Seattle, Washington. So, what is? You are. You're your own best sales asset. And "by using this communication, it invites all of us— you, me, and our clients—to show up in a more authentic way." She's sent 800 personal videos in all kinds of situations, including the pricing and negotiation impasses that inevitably come up. Often, working through the impasse means sharing bad news. For these "delicate, tricky, heartfelt" situations, Nancy says, "Video is the best." And she has a $35,000 story to support her position.

A client's brother passed away unexpectedly and, as the estate's executor, had to get his brother's home sold quickly. To help their retired parents, he wanted to get every possible penny out of the sale. Overpricing is one of the worst mistakes you can make in this situation, but Nancy had trouble getting her client to accept this fact. Even after several conversations. Because "another email, phone call, or meeting" wouldn't help her break through, Nancy got out her phone and sent a video "from the heart" (and from the car, which, as you can see in Figure 6.3, was safely parked! Never record videos while driving.).

Nancy "knew he would hear it differently than in a direct conversation." The expectation of immediate response in a real-time exchange often produces defensiveness and retrenchment into currently held beliefs and positions. "Being able to send him that communication" in a recorded video allowed her to truly reach him. Her pricing strategy was adopted and worked out beautifully, earning his parents another $30,000 to $35,000 in support of their retirement.

Visit BombBomb.com/BookBonus to hear Nancy tell this story.

FIGURE 6.3 Video Gives People Time to Process Bad News

Doing real work with real humans and achieving great outcomes is often messy and challenging. As with every other aspect of our lives, including our videos, we're never perfect. To break bad news or apologize in a way that supports constructive progress, send personal videos.

Time 7: Checking In

Problem: Attempting to reconnect or ask a favor without the benefit of your personality, failing to stand out against all the other messages people receive

Why Video: To get your face, smile, energy, and enthusiasm back in front of someone, to recreate the experience of being with you in person, to make clear your intentions

"Running into" old friends, former colleagues, past clients, and others who've made your personal or professional life more satisfying and successful doesn't have to be left to chance. You can do it at scale and on demand with simple videos. If it seems like it's been too long or you've got a favor or request to ask, video's especially helpful to control tone and express appreciation. Stay connected to people in your network, renew relationships, and spark conversations with a handful of these touches each week. Acknowledge how long it's been and express your excitement about catching up. Feel like you need a reason to reach out? Find an "in" by seeing what's new on their social media profiles.

Reading Toronto business news one morning, marketing company president, speaker, and consultant Javed Khan learned that an acquaintance was taking on a senior position at a large insurance company. He recorded a quick "Congratulations! How are you?" video and dropped it into LinkedIn messaging. Instead of getting a reply in LinkedIn hours or days later, Javed received a direct phone call from his colleague within minutes. They reconnected and caught up. The conversation quickly turned to the video Javed sent. Within a half hour of sending a personal video to rekindle the relationship, he had an appointment to present on video marketing and video communication to one of the company's executive teams.

Javed didn't reach out seeking that outcome. He didn't reach out to pitch. His video served to check in and say congratulations in a sincere and personal way. When you seek relationship before transaction, these results naturally follow.

Time 8: Internal Communication

Problem: Trying to build culture, increase motivation, and convey information with plain text, not getting enough face time with the people who drive the success of the business

Why Video: To reach remote workers, outside sales representatives, and others who aren't in the office regularly, to share information personally with everyone at the same time, to create connection and enhance culture

Many people see simple video communication as a way to convert future customers into current customers. To accelerate the sales cycle. To improve client experience. To produce repeat and referral business. And it is! But don't miss the chance to keep an internal team of people connected, informed, aligned, and motivated with personal videos.

In *The Service Profit Chain*, James Heskett, W. Earl Sasser, and Leonard Schlesinger map proven, quantitative links from internal service quality to revenue growth and profitability. They analyzed successful service organizations in an attempt to put hard values on seemingly soft measures. In these organizations, the focus is on employees and internal quality more than it is on revenue, which is an outcome, by-product, and consequence of proper focus. The links in the chain to the outcomes of profit and revenue from their source are the following:

- Internal quality drives employee satisfaction.
- Employee satisfaction drives employee loyalty.
- Employee loyalty drives employee productivity.
- Employee productivity drives value.
- Value drives customer satisfaction.
- Customer satisfaction drives customer loyalty.
- Customer loyalty drives profitability and growth.[2]

Instead of focusing exclusively on end results, focus more on their most important drivers—hiring, onboarding, training, equipping, motivating, and building into your team members. Clearer communication and stronger connection through face-to-face messages play critical roles in employee satisfaction, loyalty, and productivity. Investments in employees are investments in satisfied and loyal customers, which in turn produces revenue growth and profitability. Just as it's more profitable to retain and grow revenue from current customers than it is from new customers, retaining and building into current employees is more efficient than recruiting, onboarding, and training new ones.

As the saying goes, "people don't quit jobs, they quit bosses." Even if that's only partly true, people quit work, assignments, morale, and other factors within their managers' control. And "bosses" and "managers" are not necessarily leaders. Effective leadership is based on trust, rapport, and relationships and fosters healthy cultures and high-performing teams. If you're not communicating clearly enough, if your team's not connected enough, and if your goals, strategies, and tactics aren't aligned enough, mix some video into your communication.

In an Interact/Harris poll of 1,000 US workers, the top three issues employees have with their leaders were:

1. Not recognizing employees' achievements (63%)
2. Not giving clear directions (57%)
3. Not having enough time to meet with employees (53%)[3]

Make it a habit to send a few "thank you," "well done," or "congratulations" videos each week, as we demonstrated through leaders Brad DeVries and Todd Bland in the previous chapter. Send some of these one-to-one videos outside busy work hours to surprise and delight employees. Send some of these messages to the entire team or entire company for public praise and recognition. Send some of these to target recruits, too; you'd likely be giving valuable praise and recognition they're not getting in their current role.

After a group meeting or even a meeting with an individual, follow up with a video to reiterate the most salient points. This is also helpful for people who couldn't attend or weren't invited. You don't have to cover every detail; instead, include or provide a link to meeting notes. Steve, our CMO, does this after executive leadership meetings. For connection and alignment, a few key marketing leaders get a two- or three-minute update from him about the most important topics covered in a meeting we don't attend.

When you need to update or check in with a team member you've not spent time with recently, video helps you to be face to face when you can't be there in person. For the same reasons and in the same way that Dan Smith uses his webcam to provide his students feedback, give feedback to team members in a way that allows you to fully express yourself. These are the foundations of a service culture. It lets people know that you're paying attention, that you're appreciative, and that they matter.

In addition to these personal touches, record evergreen videos for any message you use over and over. Video is extremely useful for onboarding and training messages. Answer frequently asked questions and cover the most important topics once, then use the videos again and again as employees need them. Put those videos in drip email campaigns, YouTube playlists, training modules, and/or other places for repeated use. Share them with target recruits as a reflection of your human approach to company culture.

Time 9: Invitation

Problem: Not making clear the value of participating, not selling the opportunity with energy or emotion
Why Video: To show and tell what the experience will be like, to sell through the transfer of emotion

You're putting on an event or you're tasked with getting people to an event. Because sales is all about the transfer of emotional energy, use video to convey enthusiasm, promise value, and provide a clear call to action. What prospective registrants, attendees, or participants will get out of it is the key. Any time you put an opportunity in front of people, you have to jump the "What's in it for me?" hurdle. Blending energy, value, and persuasion in a personal, human message clears that hurdle.

This list of things to which you might invite people is not exhaustive, but it should get your mind going on all the opportunities you have to increase interest, response, and participation:

- Networking event
- Team meeting
- Company event
- Client appreciation event
- Webinar
- Training event
- Conference or trade show
- Informational breakfast, lunch, or dinner
- One-on-one meeting or appointment
- Social media connection

The video options here are not evergreen versus personal. Instead, you have the option of going one-to-one, one-to-many, or one-to-all with your video invites. As always, a truly personal, one-to-one video is most effective. For the sake of efficiency, though, you might send to a segmented list for a team meeting or training event or to a full database for a networking event or conference.

To fill up workshops and networking events, Trevor Houston with New York Life in Frisco, Texas, sends video emails. His structure is simple: energetic video, typed-out what/when/where details, and registration button. You *don't* have to memorize and deliver the date, time, location, and other specifics in your video. Instead, use one line of text to drive the video play and promise "all the details and a link to register below" in your video. The link can go to a calendar, an Eventbrite page, a webinar registration page, a website landing page, or anywhere else. When you do this with video email, segment your follow-up based on recipients' action or non-action like email open, video play, and link click. Send follow-up video emails to increase registration among those who've not yet registered and to increase attendance among those who have registered.

For one-to-one invitations, Jeff Wagner, a producing sales manager with One Trust Home Loans in Houston, Texas, uses the FORD technique to gain participation. The FORD acronym stands for family, occupation, recreation, and dreams—topics to focus on to initiate conversation. Having sent more than 2,000 videos, Jeff recognized its power to connect and convert. He decided to pick out 20 real estate agents in his area whom he *didn't* know and invite them to a coffee appointment.

Before sending each person a unique video, Jeff looked at their social media profiles to find a similarity, for example family (their kids attending the same school as his kids) or recreation (both being fans of the Houston Texans football team). In each video, he greeted the person by name, established the similarity, and invited her or him to coffee "to share ideas on how we can help each other with our businesses." He also followed up with a phone call.

With this combination of FORD, a video email, and a phone call, "14 accepted coffee appointments with me." That's a 70% success rate on invitations to people he *didn't* know. "I have my whole team doing this now and we're having success," says Jeff. "We're getting new face-to-face appointments and generating revenue. And it's because of initiating the appointment through personal videos."

Time 10: Thank You

Problem: Making sure your gratitude is truly felt, allowing your words to fall flat

Why Video: To express gratitude through tone, smile, cadence of speech, pauses, eye contact, and all those warm, human elements that are missing from text

One of the most common ways to sign off an email is with "Thanks" or "Thank you" or even "Thanks!" These are words we read on the screen so often that their sincere tone is easily lost on us. Compare that to someone looking you in the eye and saying "thank you" after you helped set aside the weight of a burden or "thanks so much" with the gleeful grin of someone who just got a raise or a referral. Think about that moment and that experience. When you can't be there in person to say or hear those words said with real emotional energy, video is the next best delivery.

In the previous chapter, we shared the benefits of expressing gratitude and saying "thank you" from a nonprofit organization and from leadership roles. Every single one of us has the same opportunity every day. Set yourself up for a successful day by starting in gratitude. Send two or three personal thank-you videos. Make other people feel good and increase the likelihood that they're there for you again in the future.

"Thank you" is one of the easiest and highest value videos to record and send. Video gives you a more meaningful touch than any other when you can't be there in person. Sincerity and gratitude are hard to capture in typed-out text or even in a handwritten note. In writing, you rely on adverbs and superlatives to convey what you'd do naturally with your eyes, face, and tone. Even if you've sent a gift basket, you've said it by phone, or you've dropped a card in the mail, a 20-second video is a simple but powerful add.

Here are a handful of times to give thanks:

- Thank you for registering on our website.
- Thanks for your time on the phone today.
- Thank you for meeting with me.
- Thanks for your inquiry, here are the answers.
- Thank you for doing me a favor.
- Thanks for who you are and all you do.
- Thank you for referring me.

- Thanks for your suggestion or recommendation.
- Thank you for making my day.
- Thanks for connecting on social media.

This 10th and final time to send video in place of text is essential to rehumanizing your business. When you make this a daily or weekly habit, you'll be glad you did. The transactional value of a "thank you" video is immense; you'll achieve more financial success when you commit to it. But the relationship value is higher. When you transcend basic give and take to celebrate the inherent value of people, you'll be successful beyond measure.

WHEN *NOT* TO SEND VIDEO

Video doesn't *always* say it better. For lightweight, transactional messages, a text or email makes more sense. Hiding a one-liner like, "Are we still on for 4 p.m.?" or "How is that project coming along?" or "Don't forget to invite Jennifer." behind a play button inside an eight-second video isn't an improvement. On the other hand, most three- to five-paragraph emails can be captured, shared, and understood better in a plainspoken video. For short and simple messages, default to typed-out text unless there's an emotional, appreciative, or subtle aspect to it that's difficult to capture in writing.

And, of course, some things are best done in person. For example, more than three-quarters of workers ages 35 and up say that the most appropriate communication method to quit your job is face to face. That share falls more than 20 points to 52% among people ages 25–34 and more than 30 points to just 44% among 18–24 year olds.[4] Shockingly, 6% of those ages 18–34 say *instant messaging* is the most appropriate way. *A* way? Yes. The *most appropriate* way? Uh . . . who's raising these people?

Think about how you prefer to learn information or receive requests. When being there in person seems best, be there in person, even at the cost of overcoming time and distance to make it happen. When that barrier is a little lower, you still want to include the richness of nonverbal communication, and scheduling a synchronous exchange in person, by phone, or by video conference is inconvenient, then send a recorded video message. Use your best judgment . . . unless you think the most acceptable way to quit your job is by instant message. In that case, ask an elder or an experienced peer.

As with any digital communication, your video may be subject to regulatory compliance, whether it's federal law like HIPAA or an internal edict from your in-house legal or security team. "Though BombBomb has passed several compliance hurdles like PCI and GDPR and continues to work toward other clearances like SOC2 Type 1," most video systems, platforms, and companies haven't done so. Use a combination of caution and common sense around information that may be subject to regulation. Do know that video email serves as an effective documentation medium. You know the exact who, what, when, and how often of every email open, link click, and video play. With BombBomb in particular, a link click can be the accessing of a document and a video play is measured second by second.

A final note on when *not* to send a video: when you've sent a lot of videos. As you're communicating with people inside and outside your organization, mix it up. Send some plain text. Send some video. Send some stylized and graphically rich emails. Send some simple, stripped-down emails. As effective a medium as video is for communication, connection, and conversion, overreliance and overuse diminishes its return. Though video humanizes and diversifies your touches, even its most ardent practitioners know it's just one part of a healthy mix.

And a final reminder on when *to* send a video: when there's emotion, detail, complexity, nuance, or subtlety involved. For example, a screen recording video may do a much better job explaining something than a set of typed-out rules and steps . . . especially with your smiling face in a little bubble in the corner along the way.

How to **Record and Send Videos**

CHAPTER 7

Sending Video in Emails, Text Messages, and Social Messages

So, you want to record and send personal videos. You've got some ideas about when to send them, who to send them to, and what to say. So how do you actually do it? Can you just record and send videos on your own? Do you need a paid subscription to a service? Should you send by email? Or Facebook Messenger? Or texting?

In this chapter, get the pros and cons of three ways to send video through email. Learn how and why you might use screen recording. Then, consider video by text messaging, social messaging, and social networks.

THREE WAYS TO SEND VIDEO IN EMAIL

Method 1: The Screenshot Method

Record, Upload, Screenshot, Link, Then Send

This method is "free-ish" and requires you to record a video, upload a video, make a screenshot, capture a link, assign the link to the screenshot, then send the email.

To send a video email, you must first record a video and host it somewhere. To focus on video for relationships rather than for marketing, we'll blow by scripting, lighting, recording, transferring, editing, and all steps required to produce a more polished video. Instead, we'll go straight to the webcam for ease and speed. Record yourself with your webcam using the default programs loaded onto your computer – Windows Camera on Windows or QuickTime on Mac. There are plenty of other webcam recorders, like VLC from nonprofit VideoLAN; they're all just a Google search away. You may also record with your smartphone or tablet camera.

At the risk of stating the obvious, most recording environments are similar. Clicking or tapping a "Record" button, which tends to be round and red, will initiate the recording. Some systems start the recording immediately, while others may count you down with a 3, 2, 1, before starting to record. In most cases, another click stops the recording. Get familiar with the most common recording environments you'll be using, so you're always ready to go. Take care to locate the camera lens, which may be hard to see if it's set against black on the face of a smartphone, tablet, or laptop screen. If you're not looking into the lens, you're missing valuable eye contact.

Once you record your video, save it on your laptop, desktop, phone, or tablet—in a folder, on the desktop, in the camera roll, or elsewhere. From there, upload it into a hosting platform. As with video recording software, numerous services can be used to host your video. YouTube and Vimeo are two of the most popular. For simplicity, let's say you upload to YouTube. Be sure to mark it as "Unlisted," because it's a video for a specific audience or person, not for open display on your channel (remember: we're talking personal video here). One way to send from YouTube at this point is to click "Share," then "Email," which sends the link in an email branded to YouTube. Of course, you could also just copy the link and share or send it however you prefer. For the more proper Screenshot Method, though, click "Share," then copy the address of the video.

Once you've got it uploaded into a video hosting service and copied its link, make a screenshot of your video's thumbnail image or of another frame in the video (slide the playbar or play and pause to find one you like). On a Mac, use "Command-Shift-4" to draw out a box of exactly what you want to capture in your screenshot. On a PC, use the Windows accessory "Snipping Tool." By controlling exactly what you capture instead of capturing your entire screen, you don't have to go into an image editor to trim it up.

Capture a frame of your video with a nice smile in it; this screenshot is your video's first impression. Bonus points for adding a play button or play bar to your image to make it obvious that clicking it will play a video. Additional bonus points for capturing an animated GIF image of your video playing with a tool like Giphy Capture for Mac or ScreenToGIF for Windows instead of a static thumbnail image. Even though they appear to have motion like a video, GIFs behave like simple image files, so they work in this method.

If you're using a traditional email marketing platform like MailChimp or Emma or if you're using a CRM or marketing automation platform, go to the email composer and place that screenshot image into your email design. Link that image to the video you uploaded to YouTube. You can do all this in BombBomb's drag-and-drop email composer, but that defeats its purpose as you'll see later in the Pro Method. Plus, we have YouTube and Animoto integrations that allow you to drop in the link alone—we'll take care of the screenshot for you. Once you've linked the image, send your email.

If you're in your transactional email inbox like Gmail or Outlook, you can do the same thing—insert the screenshot image inline in your email body. Your inbox may or may not let you turn your image into a link, so you may only be able to type it in as a text link beneath the video ("Click Here to Play the Video" or similar). Add the link however you can, then send your email.

Because you're linking to a YouTube video, an email open and a click on your screenshot or text link will send them over to YouTube. They won't be watching the video in the context of your email. And after the video is completed, they're presented with an array of other videos to watch, some of which may be your competitors' videos.

Screenshot Method Summary

- You need a video recorder.
- You need a place to host your video.
- You need to screenshot a video thumbnail.
- You may or may not be able to put the screenshot into your email.
- You may or may not be able to link your screenshot to the hosted video.
- You may need a paid service to do both of those successfully.
- Your recipient may not get a screenshot that links to your video.
- Your recipient will be taken away from your email, your call to action, and your contact information to watch the hosted video.

- Your recipient will likely be presented with other videos to watch after yours is completed.

A more advanced move is to create your own landing page that has the hosted video embedded in it. So, a click on the screenshot sends people not to YouTube, but to your own landing page. By adding this step, you give yourself more control over the video playback experience and keep your video near your branding, contact info, and call to action. Of course, that'll add even more steps and time to the process, especially if you're not using a formal email platform.

Screenshot Method Recommendation 1

If you're going to use The Screenshot Method, use a formal email platform. It'll give you open and click tracking and you'll be able to link your screenshot directly to your video. This is why this method is "free-ish" instead of free. Recording, uploading, and hosting may be free, but to do it well may require a subscription. If you do it with MailChimp (up to a limit) and YouTube, you can do it completely free.

Screenshot Method Recommendation 2

If you're going to use The Screenshot Method, focus on mass or automated sends rather than truly personal sends. It's possible to get a return on the time and effort required to go through all these steps from a personal, one-to-one send, but this method is so cumbersome that you won't create a habit that gets you to 100, 1,000, or 10,000 sends. A large audience for your video email or the repeated, automated use of your video email will provide a greater return on the effort. And most email marketing platforms are mass- or campaign-oriented, so you may not be able to easily send one to one anyway.

Method 2: The Mobile Method

Record, Then Share or Send

This method is free because you record with a device you already own and carry with you nearly everywhere you go, then share or send from that device.

This method starts in a very straightforward manner. Open the camera on your smartphone or tablet, then record a video or select one from your camera roll. Once you've got a video selected, tap the "Share" or "Email" function to send it by email. Your specific step-by-step may vary based on your phone's make, model, and operating system; if you've shared or sent a photo, your process is similar for video. Type in a little text to go with your video, then send it. Be sure to refer to the fact that there's a video to play, because it'll likely go as an attachment rather than an inline image.

As an advanced move, you can record in another app or record on your camera roll and edit in another app. Apps can be used to add a transcription, to add graphics or music, to cut in photos or other video clips, to put a fun filter on your face, or a variety of other adds and edits. Just search the App Store or Google Play for a couple of keywords around what you're trying to do (for example: "add text to my video," "video editing app," or "fun video filters"). Save this video to your camera roll, then "Share" or "Email."

Is this convenient? Relatively, yes. It requires far fewer steps than The Screenshot Method. But its benefits are limited to you, the sender, not to your recipient. And you don't get any open, play, or click tracking. Other pitfalls include:

- Upon receipt, there's no smiling face in the email (and you can't control the thumbnail image even if there was).
- Your email client has to be able to send a large attachment; our phones' cameras record very large video files these days.
- Your recipient's email client has to be able to receive an attachment that large.
- If your recipient gets the attachment, he or she has to download it in full to watch any of your video (who wants another large file saved to their laptops or phones?).
- Because you don't get tracking on this send, you can't be sure it was received.
- This one's subjective, but fair: the attachment looks and feels more suspicious and less trustworthy than a proper video thumbnail image.

With mobile cameras getting better and better in quality, the size of video files goes up and up. Videos are dramatically larger than text files, photos, and audio files. A 15- to 30-second video can be dozens if not hundreds of megabytes in size. These video files require significant upload time for you and download time for your recipient—if it can even be sent at all. Outlook's file size limit for attachments is 20MB. Gmail's is 25MB. And, again, there's no smiling face to greet the recipient to build trust and generate a play.

Mobile Method Recommendation

If you're going to use The Mobile Method, use it in high trust and high confidence situations. Getting someone to download your video to watch it requires a well-established relationship. You're asking a lot of your recipient. Getting the video through requires confidence on your part that you can send it out of your inbox and that your recipient can receive it. Because there's no tracking, you won't know if you're successful. Going device to device (iPhone to iPhone) or email client to email client (Gmail to Gmail) might help, but you've got no assurances and no feedback loop.

Method 3: The Pro Method

Record, Then Send

Many services, including BombBomb, have been designed and built to improve and align the Screenshot and Mobile Methods. Most of these services cost no more than a traditional email marketing platform and include many of the same features. Some lightweight and highly branded versions (their brand, *not* yours) are even free. A Pro Method approach to sending video email may even be built into a system you're already using.

With this method, you'll save time, improve recipient playback experience, keep your video adjacent to your call to action and contact information, and get tracking and analytics. The Pro Method keeps all your analytics under one roof—opens, clicks, plays, video heatmap, live notifications, Gmail tracking, Outlook tracking, mobile tracking, and any other data collection your system may provide. In contrast, email analytics and video analytics are in separate systems when you use a traditional email platform or CRM in The Screenshot Method.

This method eliminates or accelerates the steps required in The Screenshot Method by putting video recording, video hosting, video previewing (screenshot or GIF), and video sending all in one seamless workflow. Advantages include:

- Fewer steps are required—recording, thumbnailing, and sending are tied together.
- Video hosting is automatic and built in, not a separate tool or platform.
- Landing page is automatic and built in, so your video plays with your branding, contact info, and call to action with no extra effort on your part (exception: most free services play your video in *their* branding).

- Most services will give your video a default thumbnail image automatically, some (including BombBomb) allow you to customize the thumbnail image with a simple smile and snap of an image.
- With BombBomb, an animated preview (or GIF) of your video is automatically generated and sent in place of a static thumbnail image.

The Pro Method may also come with its own Mobile Method. For example, we provide two mobile apps for iOS and Android—one app for recording and sending videos by email, text message, and social media and another app that serves as a mobile inbox for one or more email accounts that has video, canned responses, and tracking built right in. Many pitfalls of The Mobile Method are avoided with Pro mobile apps. Videos are recorded and sent in one motion, plus . . .

- Your video's smart-streamed, rather than attached (no downloading required, just click and play).
- Your video can have an animated preview or custom thumbnail image, so you greet recipients with your smiling face, not a faceless attachment.
- Your video automatically sends in a design of your choosing.
- Tracking and analytics are included in and may be uniform across the mobile app, web app, and Gmail and Outlook inboxes.

Different tools and platforms fulfill the full promise of The Pro Method differently. Some only go part way and leave you with a link to share, for example. Too many exist and they evolve too quickly to run through them all here, but a few words on how BombBomb operates in various environments will help you determine what you need or want in your video-sending toolbox.

Google Chrome Extension

Many services operate partially or fully from a Google Chrome extension. With a click, you can open a video tool right there atop your internet browser. Typically, these extensions will provide a video recorder and quick access to the video's link, its HTML embed code, or both. The link can be dropped into a messaging app like Slack or LinkedIn Messaging. The HTML code can be used in some CRMs' email composers. From the top of your browser, you may also have access to a video library or the ability to make screen recordings.

Gmail and Outlook

BombBomb operates in Gmail through the Google Chrome extension and in Outlook as an Add In. Many other services offer one or the other. Video recording, video library access, and video sending are common features directly inside the inbox. Some go further with: tracking every email open and link click, even when there's no video; scheduling sends for any day or time in the future; selecting, saving, and reusing canned responses so you don't have to type the same email over and over or record the same video again and again; setting reminders on open opportunities; screen recording; and allowing your recipients to reply back to you with a webcam or smartphone recording. These are some of the benefits you might look for with service providers aligned with The Pro Method.

Web App Recording and Sending

Many services allow you to record and send videos from a web application to which you log in from a website. Heavier versions allow you to create emails as you would in an email marketing platform, then record a video straight into the email or insert a video into the email from a video library. Add text, graphics, buttons, and other elements to the email before sending. Lighter versions allow you to open up a recorder that drops your video into a template; add text, then send. In both cases, you can typically send to an individual, to a segmented list of people, or to everyone in your database. The ability to send designs that range from completely simple to fully designed and to send one-to-one, one-to-many, or one-to-all gives you flexibility to send videos for any occasion. Sends may be manual, triggered auto-responses, or automated sequences of emails and video emails.

Video Throughout Your Day

The Pro Method is fully realized when you have a recording and sending, access to your video library, access to canned responses and email designs, access to your lists and contacts, and tracking and analytics in a matching, unified experience across a web app, in your inbox, in a mobile app, a mobile inbox, and even integrated into your CRM or another platform. For example, a video recorder, your video library, and tracking and analytics can be used directly in a Salesforce lead or contact record. As you move from the office to an appointment, from your laptop to your smartphone, and from your inbox to your CRM, you have quick and seamless access to a consistent video toolset. This takes you beyond the one-off app, extension, or add-in to video unity and parity in the places you work every day. This is pro.

SCREEN RECORDING

Want to do an "in person" pitch, demo, or presentation, but you can't be there in person? Have a complicated web form or document that you need to walk a person through? Need to provide service or support inside a tool or platform where a customer is having trouble? Want to get someone's attention by showing his or her company website, personal LinkedIn profile, or a webinar or podcast appearance? These are just four instances in which a screen recording benefits you. Record a video of your screen as you walk and talk through slides, web pages, or anything else you have on your computer screen. But humanize it by including your face along with your screen.

The reason to include yourself with your screen should be clear by now. It's not just about the information on the screen, it's about connecting. It's about eye contact. It's about building trusting relationships at scale. If you're anxious or uncomfortable appearing on camera, know that in this situation, you're just a small image in the bigger picture. Also, we'll address that anxiety and discomfort in the next chapter (spoiler: you need push through).

Some Tips for Better Screen Recording Videos
- Include your face, not just your screen.
- Consider starting full screen on yourself with a customized whiteboard or note for a warmer introduction.
- If you don't start with yourself full screen, make sure something in the slide, webpage, document, or on screen adds specificity, curiosity, or relevance for the viewer to encourage a click to play.
- If you use more than one monitor, put the screen you're recording on your main monitor next to your camera so you can make more eye contact.
- Maintain periodic eye contact with the camera, don't just stare at the screen!
- When you make an important point, pause, look up, smile, and reiterate that point.
- Organize all the material you want to share in advance so you can just click through the slides or scroll down the page or move from browser tab to browser tab.

- Consider ending full screen on yourself for a stronger call to action with less visual distraction, unless that call to action is on the screen you're recording.

Like other styles of video, screen recordings can be used throughout the customer journey, from initial prospecting through purchase, onboarding, support, retention, and renewal. And look for opportunities in internal communication, project updates, and other situations characterized by complexity, detail, or nuance to take advantage of the additional visual support this format provides.

Some screen recording tools only capture your video, so you need to use The Screenshot or Pro Methods to host, send, and/or track your screen recording. Some Pro Method solutions have screen recording built right in. Some screen recorders don't include your face. Others allow you to have your face, your screen, or both at the same time and even to switch between them as you record. Find one that works for you and start screen recording!

SENDING VIDEOS BY TEXT MESSAGES

We were a half step away from SMS/texting while discussing The Mobile Method of video email, but the benefits of texting videos demand this breakout. Once you acquire the contact information and build the relationship, text messaging is a great way to reach prospects, clients, suppliers, strategic partners, team members, and others. Open rates, response rates, and response times are all improved compared to email. But it's also a more challenging environment.

Over the past few decades, standards have been set that allow you to successfully send one email into an incredible variety of email client, internet browser, operating system, and device combinations and produce a remarkably similar experience across them all. That animoji you sent from your new iPhone to a couple friends, one on an iPhone and one on an Android? Different experiences. Even plain, old-fashioned emojis don't display the same across devices and operating systems.

Videos sent by text message straight from your camera roll or sent as a link vary in the way they're received and displayed. For example, the direct texting of a video file from your camera roll can result in dramatic denigration of video quality to reduce its file size. Beyond that challenge of video compression, which crunches up its appearance and sound, your video may not display properly from device to device or operating system to operating system. Your odds of a clean send are best when your device and operating system match your recipient's. For example, when you text a video from your library through BombBomb's iMessage app to another iPhone, it plays directly in-line in your recipient's texting screen. Sending a link to your video, rather than sending the video file itself, is recommended.

Email laws and regulations like CAN-SPAM (US), CASL (Canada), and GDPR (EU) are well established and functionally accepted by sales and marketing professionals and by consumers. Do you have permission to mass text or even individually text your prospects? That depends on your interpretation of the Telephone Consumer Protection Act of 1991 (US). Its success depends on your prospects' and customers' expectations. In any channel, you have to provide value to be welcomed back. This is *especially* true when you text. The need for timeliness, relevance, and anticipation of your text message is heightened by the intimacy of the channel. Texting is far more personal than your email inbox or social feeds.

If your phone number and your recipient's phone number don't have an established exchange, thumbnail images or animated previews of your email may not display. Your recipient will also have an easy opportunity to block your number, just as they have the ability to unsubscribe from your email list, so treat your ability to reach that mobile number as a privilege, not as a right. Some SMS and MMS marketing systems may assign you another phone number for texting service. Be sure to give clients your proper number to reach you going forward.

A Few More Recommendations on Texting Videos

- Because of the variance in display and delivery, add some words to let people know you've sent a video and to provide a reason to play it.
- Ask a question or make a clear call to action in your video to generate a reply; tracking text opens and text video plays isn't as common or consistent as it is with email.
- When video-texting new people, focus on putting a face with the name or another concise message; respect the brevity expected in texting.
- If you sign up for a video-texting service that assigns you a new number, be sure to establish a process to give people your real, personal number if you want future conversations to move there.

SENDING VIDEOS IN SOCIAL MESSAGES

Nearly every social network offers native video features; take advantage of them. You'll get far better results uploading a video directly into Facebook or LinkedIn than you will dropping a YouTube, Vimeo, BombBomb, or other hosted link into a post or status update. Native video gets better distribution and display. They want users to stay within their social network, not follow links that send users away. They also want the video analytics. Who's watching whose videos? For how long? How often? They collect and monetize those analytics, but more so when the video is hosted natively within their platform. Most of this activity, though, is related to marketing through video or for casual communication.

When rehumanizing your communication with personal video, focus more on social messaging—Facebook Messenger, LinkedIn messaging, or direct messages in Twitter or Instagram. Rather than the one-to-anyone, anonymous broadcasting to your wall or feed, these messaging systems allow direct, one-to-one communication. A social network connection may be the only connection you have with someone, so this may be the only channel available to reach her or him. Or you may have called, emailed, and texted with someone, but this person prefers a network's social messaging to communicate with you. Regardless, personal video works well here.

- Introduce yourself to new connections and open up a conversation.
- Instead of typing a happy birthday message or clicking to congratulate someone on a new job, promotion, or work anniversary, stand out from the crowd and make the person feel special with a personal video.
- Use the "Great to Meet You" or "Check In" techniques from the previous chapter in a social message, especially if you don't have an email address or mobile number.

Sales executive and sales trainer Ronnell Richards in Atlanta, Georgia uses video to open up conversations with every new LinkedIn connection. He started recording truly one-to-one messages with the BombBomb mobile app, then dropping the link into LinkedIn messaging. Seen in Figure 7.1, this populates a video thumbnail. A connection's click starts streaming his personal video. As his presence on the network grew, however, he was connecting with as many as 50 new people every day! Because it was so effective at generating conversations, this technique required a scaled solution that preserved its personal feel. So, he records a brand new "thanks for connecting" message

FIGURE 7.1 Start More Conversations with Video in Social Messages

each morning and sends it to his assistant who uploads it and sends its link to each new connection throughout the day.

The social messaging platforms each work a little differently. Because they're always changing, we'll only briefly cover some of their differences. With the Facebook Messenger mobile app, you click the camera icon, then press, hold, and record up to a 20-second video. Releasing the button stops the recording. On your laptop, you have to break out of that little Messenger window by clicking "See All in Messenger," clicking the camera icon, and clicking "Take Video." Warning: it doesn't count you down—it just starts recording. And your limit is two minutes before it automatically stops. Your video's not available to send immediately; you'll have to wait about 60%

more time than it took to record your video for it to be encoded and ready to send (over half a minute wait after a one-minute recording, for example). And, as of this writing, you don't get a confirmation of receipt or play.

If you prefer to send immediately, drop a video link recorded and hosted elsewhere into Facebook Messenger. You have to do it that way in LinkedIn messaging—whether mobile, laptop, or desktop. They don't yet offer a recorder. Direct video messaging from the Instagram mobile app works the same as Facebook's mobile app, but you're limited to 15 seconds. To record video in Twitter's direct messaging, click the camera, then click the video icon, then press and hold "Record." The length limit is more than two minutes, but you are confined to a square. All of these opportunities should expand as we go forward.

It's worth noting that cold outreach is more difficult here. In some cases, like Twitter, you can't directly message someone who doesn't follow you. In other cases, like LinkedIn, you can reach people you're not connected to, but only if you pay for their Premium upgrade.

DELIVERY, FILTERS, AND FIREWALLS

Delivery in social messaging is pretty consistent, especially if you have a direct connection with that person. Texts will almost always go through, but links and images may be limited if you have no texting history with that number. So . . . what about email?

Mass email has legally required markings on it, like an unsubscribe link, that tell email clients that it's a mass email. If your sending domain or server has a bad reputation, your email may go to spam. No system reveals how they send email to spam. There are no hard and fast rules, even though an online search will give you some. Think of it as a demerit filtering system that blends reputation, subject line, email content, bounce rates, abuse rates, past engagement with your sends and other factors to determine where to place it. Provided you have a decent history and you're using a reputable service, a mass video email sent via The Screenshot Method or The Pro Method should perform as well as any other mass email.

Even with a good sending reputation, mass email often goes to the Promotions tab in Gmail. Some people fear this, but there's no way to avoid it. Gmail is operating in service of its customers and a mass email is a promotional email. As someone who's sent millions of emails, I don't fear the Promotions tab. Many Gmail instances, including business accounts and many mobile instances, don't have tabs at all. And only about a quarter of all emails are opened in Gmail.[1] If your Gmail recipients want to hear from you, they'll hear from you—either because they don't have tabs, they check to see what's in their Promotions tab, or they marked your emails to land in their Primary tab.

If a person says they're not receiving your mass emails and video emails, take a look at your suppression list. Your email marketing system, marketing automation system, or CRM should be keeping one for you. It's the list of all the email addresses that can't receive your email (typo in the address or address no longer exists) and people who don't want to receive your email (unsubscribes and abuse complaints). See if that person's address is on the list. If it's got a typo, correct it. If someone accidentally opted out or marked you for abuse (it happens), she will likely have to change that herself by fishing out an old send and updating her preferences. You may be able to unsuppress the address yourself.

But I'm not interested in mass video email sending, you offer. Great! By virtue of being far more targeted in your approach, your open, play, click, and reply rates will exceed industry benchmarks. On human-initiated, one-to-one sends, BombBomb strips the mass email markings on mobile and web sends (we leave them on for autoresponders and automated sequences). If you're directly in Gmail or Outlook, they're not there in the first place. With The Screenshot Method or The Pro Method, you shouldn't encounter any delivery problems.

Someone received my video email but couldn't see my video, you say. Happens. It's not foolproof. Devices, operating systems, email clients and versions of those clients, default and custom settings—there are so many variables at play. A really tough variable is the local firewall. You know the guy. Nothing bad's going down on his watch; he's got the firewall set to Threat Level Midnight! I've worked with this guy. I'd get the weekly quarantine email showing everything that got blocked at the firewall and it would be loaded with legitimate, valuable email. On emails that did go through to me, images, links, or attachments were stripped out and held behind a protective permission process.

When you identify a valuable or important domain (the part of the email address after @ that most often ends in .com), your email provider should be able to provide you or the IT person at that domain with some whitelisting information. This should get you and your emails onto the list that passes straight through the wall and gets delivered successfully. We've done this for ourselves and done it on behalf of our clients.

Here are a few hard truths. Not every video email will reach its intended recipient in the exact way you expected it to be received. Not everyone who receives your video email will open it. Not everyone who opens it will play your video. Not everyone who plays your video will respond. Chapters 10 and 11 provide very specific strategies to get more opens, plays, and replies to your video emails, as well as tailored follow-up processes. We offer this information here to remind you that video's not magic and that perfection's unachievable.

Your best bet for successful delivery is to send timely, relevant, and anticipated emails. Your personal and technical reputations are at stake. Each person's engagement with your sends will increasingly dictate when and how they receive your messages. Generically speaking, big data and machine learning inform the delivery process and decisions made favor the recipient's interests, not the sender's.

THE VIDEO VIEWING EXPERIENCE

So, my video plays directly in the email, right in the inbox?. If you're using The Screenshot Method, it's a definite no. If you're using The Mobile Method or The Pro Method, it's yes and no . . . but mostly no.

As we just established, the email inbox is a very secure environment. Many things easily executed on a web page can't be executed in an inbox. And a consistent experience is more easily delivered on a webpage viewed in one of a few main internet browsers (Chrome, Firefox, Safari, Internet Explorer/Edge) than in an inbox that isn't just accessed through those multiple browsers, but also through multiple devices, email clients, and apps (Gmail, Outlook, Apple Mail, Yahoo, Edison Mail, etc.).

Some combinations of device, operating system, email client, browser, and app will support video play directly inside the email while in the inbox. It's a function of HTML5 video support, which exists in some situations, but not in most. Apple supported it in iOS and Apple Mail for a few years, then pulled it back before partially restoring it. When and where it does work, you lose the ability to track the video play at high resolution. Many emerging, interactive aspects of email suffer this same shortcoming. To maintain a consistent and trackable experience across all the different people and environments you're sending to, BombBomb's opted to stick with the standard process of: video gets clicked, new window opens, video email dynamically appears, video plays. But we're constantly monitoring HTML5 video support and its consequences.

With a device-to-device or system-to-system match, you've got a better shot at video play in the email in the inbox. For example, if you drop a YouTube link into a Gmail email and someone opens it in Gmail, he or she may be able to play your video down in the bottom of the email. Google owns YouTube and Gmail, so they can do things like this. But if you send that same email to someone using a different service, the experience will be different.

So, "video email" may not mean exactly what you think it means as a viewing experience. But your expectations and opinions don't make it any less effective. The technology and its providers are always changing, so the standard video playback experience is changing, too. Video email and video messaging work not because of the technology but because of the humans using the technology.

FACE TO FACE IN ANY CHANNEL

If you take nothing more from this chapter, then take this: In almost any case when you're typing out and sending text, you can send a video in its place. Before you click Send, Post, or Publish next time, ask yourself, *Would this be better if I said it face to face?* In many cases, the answer will be yes. To introduce yourself in a personal and memorable way. To communicate your message more clearly. To save time by talking instead of typing. To connect with someone more effectively. To get to "yes" earlier and more often on opportunities large and small. These are the benefits of building relationships through video, and they're available in emails, text messages, and social messages.

CHAPTER 8

———

Why You're Not Sending Video and How to Get Comfortable on Camera

Overheard in small group discussions at corporate offices, conferences, team lunches, and elsewhere:

"I don't do video. Mary does video."
"Yeah, Mary does do video. I tried video. Do you do video?"
"No, I don't do video, either."

Replace "video" with "phone calls" or "email" or "meetings." Really. Replacing with "email" sounds like this:

"I don't do email. Mary does email."
"Yeah, Mary does do email. I tried email. Do you do email?"
"No, I don't do email, either."

Sounds silly, right? That's what "video" is going to sound like in the foreseeable future. Some people are more effective than others in videos, emails, phone calls, or meetings. Some people were great on their very first customer service calls or in their initial prospecting emails. But books are still written and courses are still taught about selling better by phone, sending better emails, and hosting better meetings. How long have people been standing up in front of other people giving presentations? For thousands of years! And yet we still read, write, teach, and train on presentation skills.

Our communication is constantly evolving. As it's presently evolving, video is making its way into the communication tool set of business professionals. So, let's talk about why Mary does video, but her friends don't. And how Mary and her friends can make it a successful and satisfying habit on a daily and weekly basis.

WHY WE STOP "DOING VIDEO" BEFORE WE EVEN START

You're excited and motivated to rehumanize your sales and service processes with video. Your conviction that face-to-face communication is valuable and compelling runs deep. You know video can improve results and accelerate successes. You've got a checklist of day-to-day and week-to-week triggers to go to the "Record" button instead of your keyboard. You know the various ways to record and send. You're in!

So you pick up your smartphone or flip open your laptop and fire up the camera. You look at yourself for a quick visual check. Then you look into the lens as if you're looking your viewer in the eye. You look back at yourself for a double check. And then the doubt creeps in. The fear takes over. You're in your own head. Your momentum is lost, dashed upon the rocks at the edge of an angry ocean by wave after massive wave of uncertainty.

This happens to all kinds of people who set out with the best intentions on this personal video journey: to otherwise confident and successful people, to people who have winning personalities and warm smiles, to people who build rapport quickly when they're at networking events or client meetings. It's a huge, missed opportunity. But it doesn't have to be this way for them—or for you. You need not succumb to the daunting nature of the journey, the rocks, the ocean, or the waves. They're all in your head.

We've seen it all. We've been pioneering personal video for communication, connection, and conversion with and for our customers for a decade. Along the way, we've run surveys and other feedback mechanisms to understand what stops people from adding this personal and human touch to their emails, text messages, and social messages.

Have you ever said or thought any of the following statements about your video attempts?

- I don't like how I look or sound.
- I don't know what to say.
- I don't have a system or process.

Odds are, you have. They're the most common reasons people quit before they start in earnest. So, we'll tackle these issues one by one because you're going to be using video. Soon, it'll be as standard as emails, calls, and meetings. Have some self-compassion. Get into a growth mindset. Don't listen when you tell yourself *I can't do video* or *I don't do video*. It's simply not true.

YOU LOOK (AND SOUND) GREAT

When I was a kid, we shared a driveway with the neighbors. It ran between our houses, then split out to our separate garages. Naturally, the same-age boy next door, Eli, was my best friend for several years. One of the countless creative things we did: record mock radio commercials and shows. The tape recorder my grandfather gave me was about as big as a half dozen bricks and just as heavy. The speaker took up half of the surface and the cassette tray and buttons took up the other. I'll never forget my reaction when hearing my voice played back the first time: "I recognize Eli's voice, but whose voice is *that*?!"

My coauthor had a similar experience. When he was 10 years old, Stevie got the best Christmas gift of his childhood when he opened up the Fisher Price PXL 2000. He and his friends recorded news shows and slam-dunk contests on this late 1980s video camera that recorded black-and-white video . . . on audio cassettes! Steve had the same reaction that I did. In his head, he was flying high like Clyde "The Glide" Drexler or Dominique Wilkins, whose dunks earned him one of the NBA's best nicknames: "The Human Highlight Film." On video playback, however, his sneakers barely lifted off the driveway and only for a fraction of a second. In his head, he heard Tom Brokaw or Dan Rather. On audio playback, his voice was unrecognizable to him. Who *is* that, that I'm seeing and hearing?

If you've ever recorded a personal video, you may have felt the same way!

People Already Know What You Look Like

For your entire life, you've looked out at the world from your own point of view. You approach and talk with people. You interact with everyone you seek out and everyone who comes your way. You do it all without a second thought, except for that last-minute visual check on the way out the door in the morning, that salad-greens-in-the-teeth check after lunch, and maybe that affirmational hype check before an important meeting. But something about the video camera gives you pause, when you should just be recording and sending.

As you've looked out at the world without a second thought, people have looked back at you the entire time. People already know what you look like and sound like. And for people who've never met you, your hope is that they'll know these things soon. You look like you look. And you speak as you speak. Just because you're not used to seeing and hearing yourself doesn't mean others aren't. And just because you're not recording and sending videos to people doesn't mean your appearance is a secret. Young children think they're hiding when they cover their eyes; you know better.

If a valuable prospect called and wanted to meet in an hour, you'd likely rush right to the appointment. Perhaps with a quick check in the mirror on the way out. So why keep hiding behind plain, typed-out text and passing up opportunities to get face to face? Your on-camera appearance and your message delivery won't be perfect when you start, but they will evolve as you go.

But I only work with people I'll never meet, you protest. *I don't need to get comfortable on camera and send videos to people.* This isn't about you. It's about *results.* You're going to communicate more clearly, build trust and rapport more quickly, differentiate yourself from competitors, and improve customer experience by being yourself. Whether the people you serve or sell to are spread across town, across the region, or around the world, they prefer to work with people they know, like, and trust. Asynchronous, personal videos give you a powerful way to enhance relationships, especially across time zones.

Here's the bottom line: you're your own harshest critic and you're in your own head. You're far more negative about your own appearance than anyone else is. As you're worried about a misplaced hair or a turned collar, the people attending your meeting or watching your video are worried about their own appearance, voice, ideas, experience, and success.

Through your well-manicured Facebook presence, polished LinkedIn profile, and over-crafted emails, you've grown accustomed to a high degree of control over your digital self. Giving up this level of control in favor of simplicity and authenticity is a transition you can and must make.

Vulnerability, Authenticity, and Connection

What makes video so challenging as you're getting started is precisely what makes it so valuable. Vulnerability. It can feel uncomfortable and confusing, so we avoid it. Social worker, research professor, and best-selling author Brené Brown, PhD, connects the dots on this beautifully in "The power of vulnerability," one of the most-watched TED talks of all time. Here are her logical links:

- **Connection:** It's why we're here. It gives purpose and meaning to our lives.
- **Vulnerability:** It's allowing ourselves to be truly seen and it's required for connection.
- **Shame:** It's the fear of disconnection. Our ability to feel it is required for connection.
- **Worthiness:** Feeling worthy of connection is required for connection.
- **Courage:** It's required to be who you are and to express who you are.
- **Authenticity:** It's being who you are and it's required for connection.
- **Letting Go:** We must let go of who we *think* we should be in order to be who we are.
- **Perfection:** It's unachievable. We try to perfect things and to control the outcome before undertaking an effort, but it doesn't work.[1]

Vulnerability, shame, worthiness, and courage help explain why it's hard to present our authentic selves in video. But the result—connection—explains why it's so important. Let go of the need to control how you look and sound in your videos; the control is illusory anyway. Let go of the fruitless pursuit of perfection; the reason that simple video works is that it's imperfect.

Imagine this. While recording one of your very first videos, you knock a dozen products and papers onto the floor. You disappear from the frame to pick them up, then pop back into the frame and continue recording. When you stop recording, you send it as-is to a prospective customer. As scary as that may sound, that's exactly what Steve's wife Gretchen did when she spilled her display during a personal product demo. Still uncomfortable on video, she could have stopped and started over. Instead: "Oh my gosh, I'm such a klutz. I'm sorry," she said before carrying on.

Within 10 minutes of sending that imperfect video, she didn't receive an email reply. She received a phone call. "I love that you sent that video. I'm klutzy, too," confessed the recipient. After several minutes of trading stories, her new customer concluded "I'll just buy everything." The result: a personal connection and a several-hundred-dollar order.

Our imperfections *are* our perfection. You don't get do-overs in real conversations. When you record a video, don't re-record. Send it. To get comfortable, start with videos for family members or friends. Then move on to people you work with or people you've served. These people already know and like you. You'll build up a level of comfort and work out some of the nerves. Practice builds confidence and confidence builds success. You'll learn to let go pretty quickly, especially when your efforts are validated with positive responses.

YOU KNOW WHAT TO SAY

When I hear someone say, "I don't know what to say on video," it feels like a stall tactic. When you pick up the phone, you don't need a script when the call goes to voicemail. You know why you called, so you just talk after the tone. When you run into a client downtown, you don't struggle to find words to answer his or her question. You just answer the question. When you're called on in a meeting, you offer an answer or opinion on the spot. You know what you're doing. You're a competent professional. In all these situations, you say what you need or want to say. And it's no different in personal videos.

Who are you reaching out to? Or who are you replying to? What is the nature of the opportunity or inquiry? Where is this person in the process and where do they need to go next? What do you have to teach or share? What do you need in return? This is the line of questioning you run through with anxiety before recording a video. And it's also the line of questioning you run through without conscious thought before leaving a voicemail. Again, if you're in your own head about video, you need to let go.

To help, here are a simple video fundamental, a critical mental model, and a framework for better communication.

Don't Use a Script

People love scripts. We cling to them like security blankets because they provide comfort and a sense of control (there's the "control" word again). Scripts are collected and traded in professional LinkedIn and Facebook groups. They're the basis for blog posts and content upgrades. They're dangled like carrots as a value-add incentive to pull you through sign-up forms for coaching programs and systems. They're the reason people clamored for Steve's customizable video Action Plans when we released them, even though the "scripts" were included only as points of reference to bring the Plan's dozen-plus example to life.

Use scripts as guides, not for line-by-line, word-for-word reading aloud. When you read a script on camera, it *feels* like you're reading a script on camera. Awkward and robotic. And it *looks* like you're reading a script, with little or no eye contact. Yes, television personalities read scripts written by producers and shown in a constant scroll on a teleprompter. They may not know much of what they're talking about. If you take away the script, they've got nowhere to go . . . except to commercial. It's all a production. And it takes a lot of practice, not to mention extra equipment. As with "green screen" video production, reading scripts from a teleprompter can go very badly very quickly when left to an amateur.

The Shiny/Authenticity Inversion

Here's one of the best things about personal video: it's great to be an amateur! To rehumanize your business, you're conversing and connecting, not scripting and producing. You're an expert in software, investments, education, or leadership. You don't have to be a video expert. And you may not want to be. Per a trend that's come on over the past decade, the more conversational your video is, the more approachable it feels. Polish and shine once connoted trust, but there's been an inversion, as seen in Figure 8.1. Less is more. Imperfection is perfection. Shiny is out. Authenticity is in.

But what if I want a script anyway? If you've got scripts that you picked up in sales coaching or elsewhere, read them. Understand them. Internalize them. Then put them down, click "Record," and speak the same ideas conversationally—in your own words. The effectiveness of your message comes from your confidence and tone as much as it comes through the exact words you say. Plus, if there's a particular type of video you're going to record and send often, you'll get really comfortable swapping out names, details, and other personal elements while sticking to the main structure.

If you've got a longer or more complicated video, outline it. Plan how you're going to start, know the three or four points you need to hit in the middle, and create a call to action and close. If the outline is too long

FIGURE 8.1 The Shiny/Authenticity Inversion

Shiny	AUTHENTIC
Marketing	RELATIONSHIP
Produced	SIMPLE
Scripted	CONVERSATIONAL
Edited	RECORDED IN ONE TAKE
Polished	RAW
Expensive	FREE (OR NEARLY FREE)
"Professional"	PERSONAL
From the Mind	FROM THE HEART
Formal	APPROACHABLE
Perfect	IMPERFECT
Corporate	HUMAN

to remember, write it out and keep it just off camera. If it gets awkward throwing glances off camera, keep the outline in hand and show it at the top of the video. Once people know you're working from an outline, it will be understood that you may need to glance at it once in a while. And if you do all this and still forget a detail, just include it in the text or hold it back as a reason to follow up again in the very near future.

If you want the comfort of a script for a message you've never sent, use the framework in the next section.

Empathy, Value, Call to Action

Opening with empathy, giving or promising value, then closing with a good, clear call to action is a tried and true process for effective messages. And not just in video. You can use this framework to improve all kinds of presentations and other communication.

Empathy

- Your ability to understand and relate to their feelings.
- Meeting people where they are in the process and in their lives.
- Letting them know their needs and interests are more important than your own.

Value

- Your ability to serve with knowledge and expertise and to serve as a trusted advisor.
- Trying to give them something they can't Google.
- Making tangible your unique selling proposition or differentiator.

Call to Action

- Your ability to make clear the path forward.
- Walking people through the conversion one step at a time.
- Offering the next step strongly and clearly.

By structuring your video in this way, you'll let people know why they're receiving the message, what their opportunity is, and how to proceed. More importantly, when you do this well, they'll feel great about you and the opportunity. They'll feel that you understand their situation, care about the best result for them, and can help them achieve it.

What does this actually look like? Figure 8.2 shows the script that real estate agent Kyle Williams in Cary, North Carolina used for the pre-recorded video he drops into online chats with returning site visitors who provided inaccurate contact information on their first visit. These visitors use incorrect names, numbers, and/or email addresses because they don't yet want to talk with a salesperson. The equivalent in a retail store: when the clerk asks if she or he can help you and you respond "Nope. Just browsing."

FIGURE 8.2 Example: Empathy, Value, Call to Action

OPENING	Thank you so much for visiting our website. I hope it's been a value and benefit as you're searching for your new home.
EMPATHY	I also wanted to let you know that I completely understand you not putting in your real contact information. I'd do the same thing myself if I just wanted to find a home and not be bothered.
VALUE + CTA	But when the time is right for you and you feel you need someone to help you through this difficult process, find that dream home, and get the best possible price, please put in your correct information and reach out to us. We're here to help.
CLOSE	Thanks again and have a great day!

He's right there with you; he acknowledges and understands why you gave inaccurate information ("I'd do the same thing myself"). But when you're serious, you shouldn't go it alone (guidance, access, negotiation). At that time, provide accurate information and he'll be there for you. By doing this through video instead of text, he's starting to build "know, like, and trust" earlier and faster. Because it drops the cloak of digital anonymity and creates a human experience, this type of video actively engages people who were "just browsing," accelerating the sales process.

The goal is to be approachable and conversational. People aren't hanging on your every, exact word. Instead, they're paying attention to how you make them feel. When you get fixated on saying the exact "right" words in the exact "right" order, you hinder the experience of sitting comfortably with you in person as you communicate the same message. You don't bring a script to a coffee or lunch appointment, but you know what you want to say.

So, don't read from a script. Treat your videos like you treat your voicemails—with clear intention but without a controlling chokehold. And if you need a structure, start with empathy, promise or deliver value, then make clear the next step forward.

YOUR PROCESS RESULTS FROM EXECUTION

When making the shift to video in place of some of your text, you might be tempted to imagine all the possibilities. Any message you're typing up and sending is up for video consideration. Your basis for evaluation: Would this be better if I communicated it in person? You'll find very often that the answer is "yes." When you increase all the possibilities in your consideration set, however, you decrease the likelihood of actually doing any one of them. If video is a new habit for you, incorporating it everywhere makes it feel overwhelming. You need a process. It should be simple to start and evolve over time.

Find One or Two Starting Points

From your own ideas or ideas learned in this book, choose one or two use cases. Pick one or two situations in which you say to yourself, "This is when I send a video." Then stick to it. Having one or two obvious triggers dramatically increases the likelihood that you start developing this new, positive habit. Two specific benefits to this approach:

- You'll get better and better as you record and send videos in similar situations and for similar purposes. You'll get comfortable with the recording process and you'll refine your delivery of that message, even as the names and specific details change.
- As you increase the quality and quantity of replies and results through these one or two repeated actions, you'll gain confidence and expand into other use cases. You'll start to see and be more prepared to execute on additional video opportunities.

What are these trigger points? You learned 10 of the best in Chapter 6. Be sure to review the top 10 times to click "Record" instead of typing it all out. For a quick recap and additional ideas:

- Any time you feel appreciation toward someone, say thank you.
- Any time you need to share bad news or make an apology, look the person in the eye.
- As soon as you set an appointment, confirm and set expectations.
- As soon as an appointment ends, follow up and recap key information.
- Whenever you get a prospect or client inquiry, answer the question.
- Whenever you need to provide feedback, include subtlety, empathy, and clarity.
- If someone gives you a referral, introduce yourself to the new person.
- If someone gives you a referral, thank that person and confirm you've reached out to the person he or she referred to you.
- To teach or explain, send a screen recording or face-to-face lesson.
- To show or demonstrate, don't rely on static images and typed-out words.
- When an employee, prospect, or customer changes from one status to another, support and encourage a successful transition.
- When an employee, prospect, or customer has an anniversary or hits a milestone, thank and congratulate.
- On holidays, send a mass video or several personal videos.
- On birthdays, send a truly personal video or send the same evergreen video.
- As you reach out to someone for the first time, open the relationship with warmth.
- As you advance an open opportunity, get to a yes or a no (instead of silence or a maybe) with the persuasive power of a face-to-face message.

Wherever the personal relationship and personal touch matter most to you and the people you serve, define a trigger point. Whenever you might send a handwritten note, send a personal video. Wherever you need subtlety, nuance, or sincerity, get face to face with video.

Start, Then Iterate

One of our mantras in developing this book was that you can't edit what isn't written. You can't get feedback. You can't shape or polish. You can't refine what doesn't exist. You have to get the words on the page. Execution is the key. Apply the same concept to your strategies, systems, and processes of rehumanizing your business with personal videos. Get comfortable with one or two types of videos. Get better at them. See what works. Refine them. Then add another. And another.

Only a rare few go all in successfully from the start. Vision and execution rarely occur simultaneously. More likely, you'll have a narrow starting point and grow naturally from there. Especially if you're rolling this out across a team, a measured and managed approach will be more successful. If you're a sole practitioner, you simply need to make your mind up and start doing it. If you're a leader or manager of a group of people, you're managing a culture shift in addition to a behavior change.

Successful use of video is an iterative process. Start. Observe. And refine. Your system or process is created through execution.

SEVEN TIPS FOR BETTER VIDEOS

To make that shift or change easier, here are simple tips to get comfortable on camera and record better videos.

Tip 1: Practice

If you've never done something before, but want to do it well, you have to practice. Practice is the best way to become comfortable, natural, and effective on camera. Your second video will be better than your first and your hundredth will be better than your ninety-ninth. To be clear: by "practice," we don't mean practicing without recording and we don't mean recording without sending. Record the videos and send them—even if you stumble over a word, sneeze or cough, or knock products or papers onto the floor. The quality and quantity of responses you get will accelerate the positive, upward practice-confidence-success cycle.

Tip 2: Set Your Camera at or Above Eye Level

If you're hung up on your appearance, this one'll help. Take a look at a teen in your life. When he whips out the phone, lines up the shot, and snaps a perfect selfie in under five seconds, where is his phone? Above his head, tilted downward. He holds the camera out and up for a nicer shot. Looking straight at or slightly down at yourself is a more flattering shot of your face, chin, and neck than looking up at yourself. Your goal is head and shoulders, not too tight, with room for hand gestures—all at a slight downward angle.

Arm not long enough for a nice, downward mobile shot? Get a $15 selfie stick (really). Setting up your laptop webcam shot in your office or home office? Set it up higher. Consider a $35 laptop stand, a box, or even a stack of books to help. Have an external webcam that plugs into your laptop or desktop? Set it atop your monitor or something even higher, like a shelf. And try for the corner of the room for a wider shot. Shopping for a tripod? Get one with a maximum height of 72 inches instead of 50–60 inches. Take these suggestions literally or just use them to stay mindful of where your camera is placed.

Tip 3: Look into the Lens

This may seem obvious, but many people have a tendency to look at themselves on the screen instead of into the camera lens. Looking into the lens is how you make valuable eye contact with your viewer. As you would over coffee or lunch, make regular eye contact as you speak. Don't stare the lens down throughout the recording, but also don't look down at your screen or look off at something or someone else for too long. Locate the camera lens prior to recording; it may be hard to see if it's set against a black background on the rim of a laptop or smartphone.

Tip 4: Talk to One Person

When you're sending a one-to-one video, it's easy to talk to that person directly. But when you're recording and sending a video to 10 or 10,000 people, each person watches as a single viewer. Create a personal experience. Communicate and connect with each individual. Picture or imagine one person as a proxy for the entire audience. If you struggle to do this, narrow or segment your list of recipients to unify the audience, increase timeliness and relevant for each person, and make it easier to talk just to one person.

Tip 5: Don't Use a Script

Yes, we've mentioned this before. But it's worth saying again. You don't work from a script in a voicemail, presentation, or meeting. You have a handle on the situation. You know why you're connecting and what the desired outcome is. Simply speak to it. Be conversational, approachable, and human. Use bullet points on a notepad or support yourself with visuals by screen recording. But don't type words on your screen then read them off. Not only will it feel unnatural and robotic, you'll also break eye contact with your viewers.

Tip 6: Know Where the Light Is

You don't need a professional light kit. Just orient yourself toward one or more sources of light. If you're outside, turn toward the sun rather than have it at your back. Clouds help filter and even out the sun. Standing in the shade often gives a better and more even look than standing directly under the midday sun. If you're inside, pay attention to the overhead lights, available lamps, and nearby windows. Reorient your desk so the light comes from the front or the side rather than from directly behind you. If you can't, close the blinds behind you. How is the light in the morning compared to the afternoon? Turn on extra lights to supplement when you need to. In general, more light is better than less. Steve and I both record with standard overhead lights in our offices. Steve also has a window in front and to the right of him, but I've only got a fluorescent box straight overhead.

Tip 7: Smile

"Smile before you dial," as the saying goes. And smile before you click "Record." You'll instantly be in a better mood and your viewers will confer upon you several positive attributes, even if they're not conscious of it. Smiling is a healthy habit. And it's a great practice at the beginning, at points during, and at the end of your videos. It might sound simple but think about something that makes you happy before you hit "Record." Positive thinking affects your brain, your mood, and your performance.[2]

YOU'RE NOT ALONE

Anything slowing you down or holding you back has been faced by thousands of your peers before you. And we've seen, heard, and experienced most of it ourselves.

If you don't like how you look or sound in video, that's natural. You're not used to seeing or hearing yourself. But others see and hear you all the time. Let go.

If you don't know what to say, think about what you would have typed out or what you would have said in a voicemail. It really is that simple.

If you don't have a system or process, focus on one or two common situations that benefit from a more personal touch. Know your surroundings and be ready to record whenever those situations arise. Once you've gained comfort and confidence, add in more situations.

If none of these is the issue, perhaps you're hung up on which camera to use, whether or not you need extra equipment or apps, or other technical questions. We cover all the basics in the next chapter. Spoiler: you already have everything you need to get started.

CHAPTER 9

The Salesperson's Guide
to Video Cameras

A decade or two back, only a "video person" created videos regularly and well. Cameras, editing software, and equipment were more expensive and complex. Live recording tools were few. Viewers' expectations favored full production—scripts, lights, and other specialized tools and techniques. As someone who needed or wanted a video created, you had three primary options:

1. Hire a video person or video team into your organization.
2. Contract a video person or video team from outside your organization.
3. Become a "video person" yourself in addition to serving in your primary role.

Many of those barriers to entry are gone. Video is no longer the exclusive realm of marketing departments, creative agencies, and production teams. You've got everything you need in your purse or your pocket all day, every day. Among the most prolific video users we know, their smartphones are their most-used cameras. These are people who've done one, two, or all three of the options above. With easy, inexpensive add-ons like a smartphone tripod or gimbal, a wired or wireless microphone, a lightweight LED light, or advanced camera apps, you can use your phone for almost any video. Most phones now shoot 4K or HD video at 60 frames per second. Most of them have a wide field of view and every one of them is internet-connected.

Are smartphone and webcam videos sufficiently professional for messages to your boss, your CEO, or an executive at a Fortune 500 company? Yep. We've seen countless prospecting videos recorded with a webcam and sent to directors, VPs, SVPs, and C-suite officers that generate replies and land appointments. The rise of video in social media, the democratizing effects of YouTube, and the heyday of user-generated content have lowered the bar for "good enough" production.

Furthermore, more than half a year after we published the Shiny/ Authenticity Inversion, a powerful story from the Content Marketing Institute explained how global, multibillion-dollar brands are dumbing down the quality of their marketing photos and videos in order to bring authenticity and build trust. Images are no longer perfectly posed or elaborately set. Errors and imperfections are intentional. Videos are shaky and unrehearsed. "The result is a visual style that creates a sense of identification with the photographer or videographer as a real person."[1]

While you're in your own head about whether or not your personal video is "good enough," massive and well-heeled brands with mind-blowing budgets are intentionally turning down the quality level to be imperfect, authentic, trustworthy, unrehearsed, and real. The funny thing is that you already have all those things in your favor, but you're hiding behind a keyboard. They're attempting to make "marketing through video" feel more like "relationships through video," so they're starting at a deficit compared to your sales or support efforts as an individual or team. You're already "a real person."

In this chapter, we provide the absolute basics of webcams, smartphones, other cameras, and microphones before putting them into the context of common video setups.

VIDEO CAMERA TIPS

The top camera tip we've got: start with what you already own. Your webcam and smartphone will take you a long way. When you feel like stepping up your game, that is when you could start looking at add-ons or upgrades. Don't let purchasing decisions be your excuse for not getting started today.

Webcams

Built into nearly every laptop is a high-definition (HD) webcam. Some are even built into computer monitors. If that's all you've got, start with that webcam. If you don't like the angle, prop your computer up on a stand or even a stack of books. If it seems fuzzy or grainy, be sure to turn on some lights. The resolution of most webcams is high enough that a poor image quality is more likely the result of poor light than of poor camera quality. When you use the one built into your laptop, it's with you everywhere you carry it—office, conference room, coffee shop, hotel room (for you road warriors), and beyond.

If you're wondering how "high" your high-definition webcam is, the progression of image size and quality can be seen in Figure 9.1. It applies to all cameras, so you'll see these numbers and terms when you evaluate smartphones and other cameras, too.

The more pixels in your image, the more detailed the image is. A 4K video, sometimes called ultra-high-definition (UHD), is twice as wide and twice as tall as 1080. When they're displayed in the same size viewing window, 4K looks twice as detailed as HD. 4K isn't ideal or necessary when recording personal videos; it's overkill. On the other hand, if you watch a 720-video at full screen on a 1080 monitor, it'll look a little soft and lack detail because it's scaled up. For now, 1080 HD is a good middle ground.

If you want more detail or higher quality than whatever's built into your laptop or monitor, you can buy an external webcam that plugs in by USB. There are several brands and manufacturers, but Logitech is the standard. You can get a full 1080 HD for $50 to $100 (Logitech C920, C922, C930e). For $175, I picked up a nice webcam (Logitech BCC950) with a wide field of view and a remote control to point it up, down, left, or right and even to zoom in and out. You can also go up to 4K resolution if you're willing to go up to or beyond $175 right now. Of course, all this changes quickly and there are multiple makes and models to choose from. So, don't get too hung up on specifics. Just search and browse "HD webcam" or something even more specific like "1080 HD webcam."

A webcam is great for email and social messaging videos and for video conferences. One of its key advantages is that once you get your shot setup, it's ready to go every time you need it. Have a familiar setup for your office, your home office, a conference room, or anywhere else you'll regularly use a webcam. I leave my external webcam in one spot and my laptop built-in everywhere else. Steve uses his laptop webcam all the time.

FIGURE 9.1 Comparison of Video Resolutions

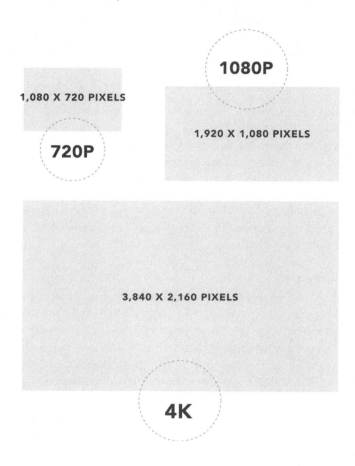

Smartphones

The camera is a key battleground in the great smartphone wars of the early twenty-first century. Each new model from Apple, Samsung, Google, and the others gets upgraded camera hardware and software as leading features. Smartphone camera specs are key talking points in ads, reviews, and comparison tables. They've evolved much more quickly than webcams.

The same resolution measures apply (720, 1080, 4K), so here's a quick take on frame rates, which are expressed in frames per second (fps). Like films in the old days, your video is comprised of multiple still images played in sequence. A higher frame rate tends to make videos look more detailed.

- 24 fps—The standard film rate
- 30 fps—The standard video rate
- 60 fps—A high video rate
- 120 or 240 fps—Rates for slow motion video

For quick, simple videos, 30 frames per second is standard. It'll keep your file size down, which makes it faster to upload and send. Some platforms don't support higher frame rates on upload or on playback anyway. As with 4K resolution, it won't hurt to record at 60 frames per second, but it's not ideal or necessary. It'll take up more space on your phone, take longer to upload, and may not be experienced by viewers.

Your smartphone's easy to operate. It's with you everywhere you go. And it's got a great video camera. If it's not your sole or primary device for video, it should definitely be in the mix.

Other Cameras

When you go beyond webcams and smartphones, you start crossing over from "relationships through video" to "marketing through video" pretty quickly. When you pick up a Canon, Nikon, Panasonic, Sony, GoPro, or another type of camera, you're committing to spend more time on your video. Offloading. Editing. Uploading. Hosting. Buying and learning additional equipment. As we established in the introduction and carry as a theme throughout the book, you can and should pursue this style of video. It can be great for your business. But its best use is for a large audience, long shelf life, or high-profile distribution.

That said, I've set up a mirrorless camera on a tripod, turned on a few lights in our small office studio, and recorded a dozen different videos for a dozen different individuals. From there, I popped out the little memory card, dragged the video onto my MacBook Pro, trimmed off the fronts and backs of the clips, batch exported the edited videos, uploaded them to BombBomb, and sent each one out to each person. Is it worth the effort? Not really.

Camcorders

Camcorders are designed for one thing: recording videos. That's their strength. Some tout an ability to capture still frames, but your phone's better. Unlike your smartphone or webcam, most have a proper lens system that allows optical zoom (rather than digital zoom, which just enlarges the image and reduces its quality). Most can be mounted directly to a tripod or held in the palm of your hand. Most have plugs for external microphones and can have a small light mounted atop it. Many come with remote controls, which is helpful when recording videos of yourself. Most have flip-out screens and automatically help stabilize handheld shots. Unlike the next two camera types we'll cover, camcorders can record for an hour or two straight—uninterrupted, all in one clip. This makes them great for recording presentations, speeches, trainings, team meetings, and similar.

Target: $400–$1,200 (any less and you should stick with your smartphone, but for any more you should look at the next two categories)

Digital Single-Lens Reflex (DSLR) Cameras

Essentially a digital version of the old 35 mm film cameras, the digital single-lens reflex (DSLR) camera category is led by Nikon and Canon. DSLRs are excellent for still photo images and quite good for video. Their advantage over camcorders is the versatility that comes with your ability to change out lenses—wide angle, telephoto, zoom. Not all lenses work with all DSLRs. When you commit to a brand, you're committing to an entire lens ecosystem, so do your homework.

Here, image quality is derived from lens speed and glass quality. You can buy a very expensive camera body but be disappointed with the image quality if you put a cheap lens on it. Most video streamed on the web has reduced sharpness and image quality, so this may not be noticeable. Fast, high-quality lenses can give you a beautifully blurred background that feels very polished. Do a Google image search for the word "bokeh" and you'll know the look. If it's in your budget, get nice lenses.

Like camcorders, most DSLRs mount directly to a tripod, have plugs for external microphones (a must-have feature), include image stabilization, have flip-out screens, and directly support a mounted light.

Target: $600–$2,400 (plus another $1,000–$3,000 for lenses)

Mirrorless Cameras

To the video layperson, these look identical to DSLRs, except their bodies and lenses are smaller and lighter. But there's a big difference inside the camera body that gives a mirrorless camera a video advantage. They're not the digital version of the old 35 mm film cameras that use a mirror to reflect the light that comes in through the lens up to a sensor. The light goes directly from the lens to the sensor because they're . . . mirrorless! One important consequence of this design is that autofocusing, face detection, and eye detection while recording videos is superior to the DSLR.

Beyond this, they have most of the same features and advantages of a DSLR. The only downside is that battery life may be a little shorter for perpetual reliance on the screen or the electronic viewfinder to display the shot's subject. Sony, Panasonic, and Olympus have led the way in mirrorless cameras, but all the main manufacturers, including Nikon and Canon, are in the mirrorless game.

Target: $999–$3,500 (plus another $800–$2,400 for lenses)

For more camera types and links to examples, visit BombBomb.com/BookBonus

Microphones

Low image quality is more tolerable than low sound quality. As with cameras, use the microphone you have right now until you reach its limits. Your laptop or webcam has one built in. Your smartphone has a great microphone because it's actually a phone; it's designed to be talked at and spoken into! Don't use the fact that you've not researched, shopped for, and purchased a microphone as an excuse not to get started with personal videos.

Before you buy an upgraded microphone, use these tips:

• Bring the mic as close to you as possible while still keeping a head and shoulders shot that also captures some hand gestures.

- Use your wired or wireless smartphone earbuds to capture sound for your smartphone videos—or even your laptop videos.
- Get great sound with just a single Apple Airpod; they connect wirelessly both to iPhones and Androids.
- If you don't like the "earbuds in the shot" look, hold the earbud mic immediately out of the shot as near to your voice as possible.

In case you still want an additional microphone, we'll cover two main types: USB and 3.5 mm jack. It's not as technical as it sounds.

To upgrade the audio from your laptop or desktop computer, look for a microphone that plugs in by USB. In the $50 price range, take a look at the Samson Meteor or Blue Snowball. There are others, but we use and like both. The Meteor is especially portable. Another standard is the Blue Yeti, which is priced around $125. Before you go down this road, know that most external webcams like the Logitech models mentioned earlier come with microphones that are better than your built-in. You don't necessarily need to buy a USB mic until you've tested the sound with your upgraded webcam first.

For smartphones and other cameras, you'll look for the standard 3.5 mm jack—that short, skinny plug that's silver, copper, or gold in color and/or material. Until Apple moved to their proprietary lightning jack, all these devices used this size. For iPhone or iPad, you'll use the lightning-to-3.5 mm adapter they provide or get one that's already lightning compatible.

The wired lavalier microphone plugs into your smartphone or camera and runs over to you. It's typically clipped to your clothing, high up on your chest near your voice. The little foam ball on it helps reduce wind noise and those pops we make when we enunciate words like "pop!" These work well when you're still, the camera's still, and you're near your smartphone or other camera.

You can also buy a wireless kit, but then you've got two separate battery-powered packs that need to be synced up. One pack attaches to you; its wire runs up and the mic gets clipped near your voice. The other pack attaches to the camera, gets your audio wirelessly, and passes the sound into the camera. This allows you to move around a bit more. Wired or not, a single lavalier microphone is passable but not ideal for two-person interviews. It's better if each person has one. Wired and wireless handheld microphones are better for interviews, but they can look very old-fashioned.

To capture sound from more than one person and to avoid having the mic attached to anyone, a camera-mounted microphone is a good option. Small ones are made to attach directly to smartphone. Larger ones are made to mount directly to your camcorder, DSLR, or mirrorless camera with a standard shoe mount. Look for one that allows you to switch from the standard foam cover to a "cat tail" or "wind buster"—that big, gray, and fuzzy cover that's crucial for outdoor use. The fuzziness and hairiness dramatically cuts down wind noise, which can ruin your sound. Some of these mics are even boom-mountable, so they can be held out of the shot but closer to the people who are speaking.

VIDEO SETUP TIPS

To provide a little more context and specificity to camera and microphone considerations, here are three of the most common video setups. The importance of being set up and ready is that it greatly increases the likelihood that you'll actually record and send a video when you know it's the right thing to do. You're more likely to get out the door for a run if you know where your running shorts and shoes are. And even more likely if you have them on!

The Office Setup

At a desk or in a cubicle. In an office or home office. This is the spot where you set up once and use it over and over again as needed; see some of the typical equipment in Figure 9.2. It's a familiar and comfortable space. Personalize the background with artwork, photos, trophies, diplomas, plants, or anything

FIGURE 9.2 Be Ready to Record in Your Office

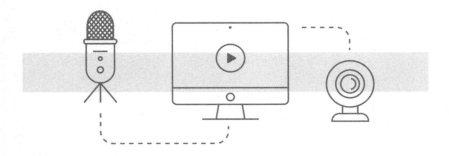

else that communicates that this is your unique space. There's so much people can learn about you from your office; it gives you the opportunity to tell a story about yourself.

Recommendations for Your Office Setup
- Keep the space basically tidy. Your background should help communicate who you are; make it personal, but professional.
- Your go-to camera here is your webcam, even though your smartphone is an option.
- Add a USB microphone if desired.
- Rely on all available natural light coming in from a window or an open door. Notice how it changes throughout the day.
- Supplement your lighting with overhead lights, a clip-on desk lamp, or a floor lamp. You might use this lamp or light only when recording videos.
- More light is always better than less light.
- Place your external webcam higher up and in a corner for a nice, wide shot. Use a bookshelf, wall shelf, or tripod for height.
- Place your built-in laptop webcam on a laptop stand, box, or stack of books to raise it up.
- Especially for live recording, a hardline internet connection is better than a WiFi connection.

The Mobile Setup
A perfect video won't convert more leads. A little handheld shake in your video doesn't mean you can't send it. Mixing up your locations by being mobile keeps video communication interesting for you and for your viewers. Being prepared to record with your smartphone means you're always prepared, because it's with you almost everywhere you go. As you see in Figure 9.3 and in the list below, you augment the arm-out selfie experience with add-ons.

Recommendations for Your Mobile Setup
- If your arm isn't long enough to produce a nice, wide shot, get a selfie stick.
- Walking and talking provides visual interest. Use a device like the DJI Osmo, Osmo Mobile, or another mobile gimbal to steady the shot.
- The cheap solution for walk-and-talk videos is to record with the Hyperlapse app, but save the video at 1x speed instead of at a 6x or 12x lapse speed. It stabilizes the video. Or search for another stabilization app.

FIGURE 9.3 Be Ready to Record with Your Phone

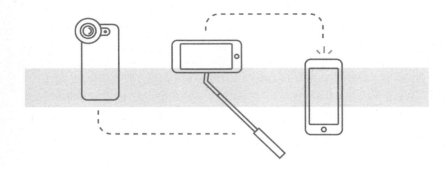

- If you don't want to stick with your wired or wireless earbuds, search for a mobile microphone. Search "mobile microphone" or "iPhone microphone" or "Android microphone."
- Sitting safely parked in a car is a great place to record. You often have good light and good sound. If you're an on-the-go salesperson, this is a great way to spend those five or 10 minutes between meetings.
- If you want to set your smartphone in one place, get a mobile tripod head and use it with a small or full-sized tripod.
- Countless apps are available to edit your videos, add graphics, add transcriptions, and more. Just remember to focus on speed over production.
- If you're using a video email service provider, that company should offer mobile apps for recording, sending, and tracking.
- If you're on the move, consider recording straight to your camera roll, then uploading once you're on a stable, solid internet connection.
- A WiFi internet connection tends to be faster and more stable than a cellular connection.
- If you're on the move, pay attention not to drop off WiFi by moving out of its range.
- If you're on the move, especially as a passenger in a moving car (do not drive and record!), know that cellular connections can drop your video like they drop your calls.

Note: Our mobile apps provide some protection from that last scenario. If you drop connection between cell towers, we pause the upload, then automatically resume when the signal picks back up.

The Pro Setup

Again, we're creeping into "marketing with video" territory, but we expect you may want some tips on a more traditional or "professional" setup pictured in Figure 9.4. And some of these ideas are transferable into "relationships through video" scenarios. We'll focus here on a simple setup in a small office or as a smaller part of a much bigger space.

Recommendations for Your Pro Setup

- You can use a webcam or smartphone on a tripod, but this setup is best with a camcorder, DSLR, or mirrorless camera.
- Get an on-camera microphone, a boom microphone, or a lavalier microphone to plug into your camera.
- If you experience echo, the space has too many hard surfaces that bounce sound and too few soft surfaces that absorb sound. Add soft surfaces like area rugs, pillows, blankets, soft-sided chairs, foam blocks, or similar. It doesn't have to be pretty if it's not in the shot.
- Use a plain colored wall, a tradeshow booth backdrop, a sign or logo, or another relatively clean background for your shot.

FIGURE 9.4 Studios Are More for Marketing Videos

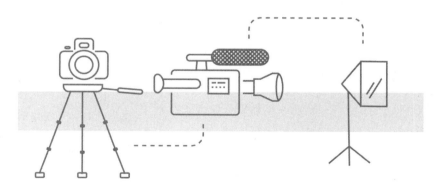

- Do not stand directly against the background. Create some distance. In a tight space like an 8′ × 12′ room, use the shorter wall as the background so you have the longer wall for depth. You can also shoot on an angle into the corner.
- Search for a three-light kit. Two good options include LED lights that are dimmable and with a sliding color temperature or a kit with at least one soft box.
- If you're not familiar with lighting a shot like this, search "three-point lighting." Look at some diagrams and watch a video or two. It's very straightforward.
- Get a tripod. Look for more height rather than less (70″ or 72″, not 50″ or 60″). If you're not going to leave it up all the time, take note of how well it packs down. If you're primarily using it for locked-down shots, don't worry too much about panning and tilting fluidity.

THE RIGHT TOOL FOR THE RIGHT JOB

The goal here was to provide a basic overview of equipment considerations to record videos reasonably well. Your goal is to use the right tool for the right job. If you're sending a Gmail video reply to answer a customer's question, just click "Reply," click "Record," then talk to him or her through your webcam. If you're recording a video for an email being sent to 27,464 potential customers, you can still get away with your webcam, but you'd also be justified in going over to the 8′ × 12′ video recording room, turning on some lights, and firing up the camcorder.

Even if you're an absolute novice when it comes to video equipment, the basic answers are just a search away. Reading product reviews and watching how-to videos provides knowledge, but comprehension and application only come through setting up and recording some videos. You already own what you need to get started.

▶ PART

4

Improving **Video Results**

CHAPTER 10

How to Get More Opens, Plays, and Replies

Sending video tends to yield better results than sending plain text. But it's not automatic or guaranteed. A little thought, intention, and care goes a long way toward better outcomes. In this chapter, we'll explore the leading causes of poor email results and best practices to get more emails opened, to get more videos played, and to achieve your desired outcome more often. If some of the language sounds too deeply rooted in sales or marketing, know that these principles and practices can be used in any context.

TOP REASONS FOR VIDEO EMAIL UNDERPERFORMANCE

If you put email on autopilot, pushed the "set it and forget it button," let other people write your emails, let machines shoot them out, and just sat back waiting for replies, you may have made a costly mistake. According to recent research from the Relevancy Group and One Spot, email marketing's contribution to company revenue is up two percentage points to 20%, more than 10% growth year to year. Open rates and click rates are also up two points each, to 27% and 16%, respectively. And among companies using personalization, conversion rates increase 6% and average order value increases 5%.[1] Because millennials use email more than any other generation, this trend will continue.

Whether you're looking to directly drive revenue or trying to communicate more effectively, a little effort can make a big difference. Before sharing specific strategies to increase email opens, video plays, and overall conversion, we've got five specific reasons emails and video emails underperform.

It's Not Sincere

Sending selfish emails based on your interests instead of your recipients' interests is the easiest thing to do. As a consequence, it happens often. We've done it ourselves. And we expect you have, too. Before starting on an email, video email, or video message, ask yourself, "What's the benefit to the recipient?" Every message you send trains people to open or delete your next message. If there's no clear benefit, value, or sincerity in the message, you're failing to positively reinforce the next open. Employ the Empathy, Value, Call to Action framework introduced in the previous chapter to overcome this common weakness.

> Every message you send trains people to open or delete your next message.

As you well know by now, sincerity, service, and passion come through much more effectively when you deliver it through video. These are qualities we can *feel* through nonverbal communication. And they're incredibly difficult to capture and convey in typed-out text.

It's Not Clear

Within 10 seconds of opening your email, a person should have a strong sense of why you sent it to him or her, what the opportunity is, and how to proceed. It should be set up with the subject line, sketched out in the email body, brought to life with your video, and closed down with a clear call to action. That action might be a reply, a click, a call, or any other means of proceeding on the offer you present.

The video and text portions should be aligned and complementary, *not* redundant. Your text should help drive the video play. The video's job is to humanize the message, build connection, and persuasively drive that one, clear call to action. People are too busy and too distracted to deal with the friction of rambling or unclear emails, multiple calls to action, or a call to action that isn't clearly set up.

It's Not Targeted

If you don't send emails to lists of people, jump ahead to the next section. If you do send mass messages, this one's critical, especially with video email. Because in video your reputation isn't just tied to your name, email address, and logo. It's also tied to *you*—your face, voice, and personality!

Whether it's a preference for vanity metrics, a transactional mindset that's satisfied with 0.6% conversion on volume, simple laziness, or another reason, mass emails are often sent to too broad a group of people. You might select everyone and click send. Or you might write an email for a specific persona or purpose and use it outside those bounds. Either way, it hurts to send without intention. It's like the Boy Who Cried Wolf. It only works a couple of times before we catch on.

Narrowing your list by segmenting and targeting down to a more appropriate sub-list of recipients will drive up successful delivery, open rates, play rates, and response rates. You don't have to get too complicated with it, just be mindful. Any damage to your ego done by the smaller "send" count will be more than repaired by the lift you'll see in short-, medium-, and long-term results.

It's Not Tracked

The goal isn't just to send the video email or video message. We don't pat ourselves on the back for getting it recorded and clicking "Send." The goal is to create conversation and get to "yes," whether it's a micro-yes like a simple click through an email or a macro-yes like a signed contract. Tracking closes this gap. This is one of email's great advantages over other channels and the source of its incredible return on investment. You know exactly who's interested based on their actual behavior. Follow up one-to-one or one-to-segment messages based on who did or didn't open, play, or click. Understand what the behavior or non-behavior means relative to the opportunity you provided, then speak to it. The send is the start. The tracking tells you how to proceed. Especially with video.

A video play is the ultimate gauge of interest and form of engagement. A one-second glance or accidental touch of your email can trigger an email open. But when people give you 45 seconds of their time and experience you in person, they show real interest. Wouldn't you like to know that? What if someone watches you for 87 seconds on a follow-up send? It's a great indicator of the growth of "know, like, and trust." Pay attention to who's watching and when to know where your best opportunities and greatest interest are. You don't know who those 529 people who watched your YouTube video are, but you know *exactly* who played the video in your email.

It's Not Differentiated

With the same black text on the same white screen, your email looks like his email. And his looks like her email, which looks almost identical to their emails. And all of our emails look the same as they did five or 10 years ago. For some sends, that may be just fine. You already have the relationship. The information is concise and easy to understand; it's not hard to capture in text. But when you need to really differentiate, connect, and convert, you need video. Sure, your signature or your header has a different color, logo, or headshot, but when your recipient is plowing through a couple dozen emails in a single pass, that's no longer enough.

If you and I took the exact same typed-up email message and each delivered it in a video, our videos would be completely unique. You'd deliver it differently than I would. No one else can send the same video email as you. You're not one in a million; instead, you're one of a kind. You are the differentiator, so differentiate and rehumanize by blending some videos into your business communication.

HOW TO GET MORE EMAIL OPENS

Entire books have been written on this topic. Webinars, blog posts, and studies have been produced on it, too. But we'd be remiss in failing to address this topic, because your video can't be played without your email or message getting opened. The primary factors affecting whether or not your email gets opened include the following:

- Your "From" name and "From" email address—trust symbols that, ideally, are recognizable to your recipients
- Your subject line—clear and concise or compelling and curious
- Your targeting or segmenting—if you're sending to more than one person
- Your history of sending to that person—your consistent delivery of value, their enjoyment or appreciation of your past sends
- Sending day and time—if you have options besides "right now"

There are no universally applicable answers here. A search for "best day and time to send email" will give you plenty of confident results, but they're also contradictory. What works for one person's or company's recipients may not work for yours. If you're sending prospecting, sales, or marketing emails to individuals or to lists, pay attention to the tracking and analytics provided by your system to see if there are any over- or underperforming send days or times.

The "From" name and "From" email address show up with your subject line. According to a deep roundup of email stats by MarketingProfs, 68% of Americans open based on the "From" name and 42% of people around the world look at the name to decide whether or not to open. This ability to identify the sender is a top trust factor for your recipient.[2] We recommend that emails come from a person, rather than a generic address (office@) or the dreaded "noreply@," and that the "From" name and "From" email address match. For example: Ethan Beute, BombBomb or Ethan at BombBomb for the "From" name and Ethan@BombBomb.com as the "From" email address. People like to do business with people, so being personal and specific about who you are helps performance across the board.

When you're consistent in your "From" name and address as you reach out to people over time, you're building a reputation with that person. But you're also building a relationship between your email address and sending domain and each recipient's email address and receiving domain. They're shaking hands and getting to know each other as your recipient opens and engages with your email and especially when you reply back and forth. This feedback loop of how well your emails perform with each person will increasingly dictate your access to inboxes in the years ahead. So, take care to send relevant messages to each person and build a history of doing so.

The most easily observed and controlled factor here is the subject line. One route is being clear, direct, and specific. Another is creating a curiosity gap. With the former, make it clear that what's inside is relevant and valuable to each person who receives it. This is easier to do when it's for one specific person; the goal in that circumstance is to make clear not just that it's relevant and valuable, but also that it's specifically for him or her as a unique individual. With good segmentation or targeting, you can write to the commonalities that tie those people together to assure relevance and promise value. The commonalities may be based in the nature or source of their inquiry, a behavior they've taken in the past, their purchasing history, their status or relationship to you or your organization, or any of a variety of other factors you used to segment.

The latter, creating a curiosity gap, involves starting a story or a line of thought in the subject line that continues inside the email. If you're sending from a platform that allows you to add preheader text, you can use that to start the story, too. The gap is the mental distance between what we know (provided in the subject line) and what we need or want to know (awaiting inside the video email). You're tapping into FOMO, or "fear of missing out." This is a subtle art, not a clickbait hack. Consistency between what people expect to get based on the subject line and what they receive when they open is important to building trust and earning the next open. Add a sense of urgency to heighten curiosity (example: two reasons you shouldn't wait to open this email). Go counter to what we know or expect to spike curiosity (example: two reasons not to open this email and one reason you should).

How long should your subject line be? If you search that online, a number you'll see often is 50 characters. But the real answer is . . . it depends. One of many useful ideas presented in *The Rebel's Guide to Email Marketing* by Jason Falls and D. J. Waldow is that shorter subject lines tend to produce more opens but lower engagement inside, while longer subject lines tend to produce fewer opens but higher engagement inside.[3] When you spell out more clearly exactly what's inside, fewer people will take you up on it, but they're the "right" people. The point here: your open rate is only one measure of success and it's not necessarily the most important one.

And what about the word "video" in the subject line? We've seen all kinds of impressive, if not exaggerated, numbers thrown around. In our own analysis of 15 million emails sent in a one-month period, including the word "video" in the subject line increased open rates by 8.3% and increased video play rates by 32.8%. Being clear about what's inside gets more of the "right" people into the email and interacting with it.

HOW TO GET MORE VIDEO PLAYS

Your video thumbnail image or animated preview is to your video play as your subject line is to your email open. It's not the only factor involved, but it's an important one. It's your video's first impression. As with your subject line, use the thumbnail or animation to help people know that the video is just for him or her as an individual or that it's relevant and valuable based on a specific, common factor shared with other members of a segmented group. Things you may include in your thumbnail or preview:

- Your smiling face with a hand wave and/or a gesture to a whiteboard or note
- A whiteboard or note with his or her name on it (example: Answers to both of your questions, Jeff!)
- A whiteboard or note with a detail that's true of or interesting to recipients (example: Now that you've signed up for the sales training . . .)
- A whiteboard or note with a specific promise of value in the video (example: Click play for three ways to save time and make quota this month)
- A whiteboard or note with a question on it (example: Wondering why you're not getting more calls back?)
- A background that's visually interesting, has movement, or relates to the video content (example: walking down the street, riding an escalator, standing in front of a crowd or activity)
- A background with highly relevant or self-identifying information on the screen in a screen recording video with your smiling face inset (example: a prospect's website, LinkedIn profile, or a podcast, webinar, or blog he or she was in)
- A display of the video's length, especially when it's under one minute, to manage expectations (some services, including BombBomb, automatically display this)

An animated preview provides additional visual interest and has stronger connotations of video than a static image. Together with the video duration display, a study we conducted showed a 48.9% increase in video play rates compared to static thumbnail images.[4] The addition of a whiteboard, sign, notepad, sticky note, or another place to write a message specifically for the recipient or specifically about the video's content creates curiosity or promises value, further motivating the click to play.

Another important factor is your video's relationship to the text in the email body. We discourage sending video on its own with nothing else there to support it. And we caution against the natural tendency to reiterate in the text exactly what's said in the video or vice versa. Reading the email body should be a unique and complementary experience to watching the video.

With this in mind, include at least one line of text in your video email. It should take on two jobs at once: letting the person know the video email is just for her or him (or at least relevant to her or him if you're sending to a list) and giving one reason to play the video. Sell the value of the video in one or two lines, the same way that you sell the value of the email contents in the subject line. As an added benefit, emails with just 50 to 125 words get 50% higher response rates than emails with more typed-out words, according to that MarketingProfs email roundup mentioned earlier in the "From" name discussion. You're about to get some proven practices for getting more responses, but first we'll answer a common question.

HOW TO KEEP PEOPLE ENGAGED IN YOUR VIDEOS

Have you ever walked by a puzzle that's nearly complete, but two or three pieces are still missing? Most people feel the urge to pop those final pieces into place. The Zeigarnik Effect suggests that our brains have a strong desire for us to finish what's been started. Play to that human instinct by promising a specific number of topics, tips, or ideas that you're going to cover in your video. You could include this in the subject line, email body, and the animated preview. Make the promise off the top of the video, then count them off as you go. As in: "Hey, Mike! I've got three important details for you in this video. First . . ." When Steve uses this tactic, he likes to make the first topic especially quick to create a sense of progress—that feeling that it's moving along quickly.

If you don't want to create a numbered sequence, you've got some other options to draw people through your video. You can start by introducing a potential, better future for the person, then backing into what needs to happen to get there. You can structure it as a story by setting the scene, identifying the characters, talking through some action, getting to the crux or climax, then winding down to the resolution. Or you can go with this classic structure: "Tell her what you're about to tell her, tell it to her, then remind her what you just told her."

Do not bury your call to action or best promise of value at the end of the video. No matter how well you do it, some people won't make it to the end of your video. That's normal. Some people don't answer your call or show up for your appointment. Weave the top takeaways through the entire video. Think of it this way: "tell him what he should do, tell him why he should do it, then remind him what he should do."

HOW TO INCREASE YOUR REPLY RATE

The single most important thing you can do to increase people taking you up on your call to action, whether that's a reply, a click, or another behavior, is to ask for it. Make it clear and make it easy. Any complication, confusion, or other friction that is introduced clouds the main message and makes it more difficult to proceed with you. Again, each person should know in a quick scan why they received your message, what the opportunity is, and how to take you up on it.

Beyond a direct email reply or link click, your video system may provide additional ways to reply or otherwise engage. Some systems allow you to set up clickable calls to action on top of the video (think: YouTube popover boxes). Others allow you to have clickable items around the video. BombBomb offers people who play your video the opportunity to like it with one click, to reply through an open text box adjacent to the video, or even reply with their own video. All three come back as messages in your inbox.

So what motivates the reply, click, or other forms of engagement? Recording and sending a truly personal video triggers a sense of reciprocity, one of Dr. Robert Cialdini's 6 Principles of Persuasion, because time is an asset.[5] You're demonstrating in an obvious and meaningful way that you're giving your time and attention directly to that person. A reply is almost obligated. Acknowledging commonalities or similarities triggers liking and the formation or strengthening of a social bond.

Especially for consistent webcam shots in your office, home office, or someplace else, you can enhance liking and bonding by including personal elements in your background. This might be a family photo or another visual sign of who you are and what's important to you. As you can see in Figure 10.1, Steve has a drawing of his three children, a small collection of vintage cameras (ask him about it when you see him), and a trio of paintings that suggest you "Explore," "Be Kind," and "Be Brave."

After completing a transaction with a client, salesperson Ken Mucha in Bend, Oregon, received the following email:

FIGURE 10.1 Steve's Office Helps Tell His Story

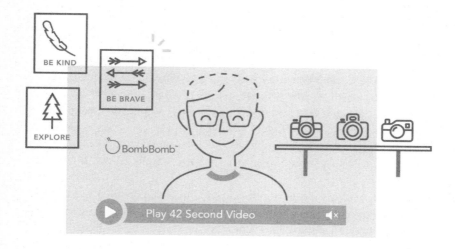

FIGURE 10.2 Ken's Office Helps Tell His Story

Hey Ken,

I'm just cleaning out my mailbox and wanted to share a few thoughts with you.

Your videos were a major reason I chose to have you as our Realtor. After watching your first video, then reading the reviews from your customers, I had this comfortable feeling that I was doing business with a friend.

I loved seeing your kids' art posted on your walls. I remember when our kids were young and their masterpieces covered our walls. I've spent my career in sales, and you do all the little things right.

I look forward to talking with you soon.

The little things make a big difference. As seen in Figure 10.2, Ken sends webcam videos from his office; he's sent nearly 4,000 videos in total. On the board behind his desk are coloring sheets from his kids. It's not a tactic. It's who he is. He becomes more relatable simply by being himself in his natural setting. These little things add to your presentation style and make your videos feel more personal. It's pretty easy to make a truly personal video feel, well, personal. But what about messages to larger groups of people? Talk to one person. Rather than "Hey, everyone!" try "Good morning!" or "Happy Thursday!" as the opening to your video.

> Video isn't just a tactic. It's who you are. And it's a moment of your day.

Being personal increases connection and compliance. If you're up for some experimentation, though, try a proven concept like "because." In a classic psychology experiment, providing even the most basic reason (not even a good one!) increased compliance with a request by more than 50%.[6]

Or tap into social proof or scarcity, two more of Cialdini's Principles of Persuasion. With the former, mention your online reviews or how you've helped other people in your prospect's situation. You could even share a video testimonial from a client you served in a similar situation. For the latter, be sure to mention any limited aspects of the opportunity you're presenting, like time or quantity. A quick search around sales psychology will provide you hours of additional reading and many more tips like these.

One of the best things about prospecting with video is repetition. You'll get to work these ideas out over and over again every day. You'll develop some structure or phrasing in your video with which you're more comfortable; you'll find your flow. Try one of the ideas mentioned above for a few days. What did you change and when? Did you notice any qualitative or quantitative changes in response? Take notes along the way so you're not exclusively relying on your impression or memory. Even a light commitment to systematizing your approach in video can heavily influence your response rates. And if you're on a team, share your findings with each other.

As mentioned earlier in this chapter, provide one clear call to action. Set it up in the subject line and reinforce it all the way through the entire video email to make it far easier for each person who receives it to take that next step. Don't provide too many options, either. If your goal is an appointment, try, "Does tomorrow at 4 p.m. or Friday at 10 a.m. work better for you?" in your video and email body rather than, "Would you like to schedule an appointment?" If your goal is a click-through to a calendar, event registration, landing page, or someplace else, make sure the button or text link is prominent. If your goal is a reply, ask for it. Support that ask with a "because." And if you see you've received an open and a play but no reply, reach back out.

TIPS FOR PROSPECTING WITH VIDEO

Introducing yourself to someone you've never met is one of the most valuable ways to use personal video. It drives a significant increase in replies, especially when paired with phone calls. When you lead with the video, then call based on your analytics and alerts, you can even eliminate cold calling. When you see your video's been played you know he or she has "met" you through video, so it's a great time to pick up the phone. Because this movement is still in its early stages, the video alone will set you apart. But as personal video becomes more common, your mastery of it will keep you ahead. Here's an example, followed by best practices for adding this more personal touch to your prospecting.

Our team created opportunities for 12 companies to participate in a pilot program to test and measure the benefits of adding video to their sales processes at no cost. The team identified ideal companies based on their tech stack and its match to the BombBomb system and started to reach out. Figure 10.3 shows a send from Enterprise Solutions Director James Stites and its result.

Notice how he brought together several of the elements we've already recommended, including:

- A little curiosity gap and personalization in the subject line
- More curiosity and personalization, plus a promise of value, to drive the personal video play
- A very clear line of thought to drive the call to action
- One link to click to schedule the intro call

The structure, message, and targeting worked together to drive his desired outcome with 20 minutes of sending. Here's the reply James received: "James – I like this! I will schedule a time, but I need a couple of other people to join us. Can you send me dates, times for early next week and I will coordinate?" Not bad for a first touch!

The End of Cold Calls

"I hate cold calling more than anything in the world." Can you relate? It's a confession of George Schramm, a mortgage professional who's eliminated cold calling from his life. Numerous times he's warmed up relationships by introducing himself to people involved in a transaction whom he's never spoken to, to top producing real estate agents he's never met, to unresponsive leads in his database with whom he's never directly connected, and in other cold situations. With new real estate agents, for example, he either reaches out based on one or two mutual acquaintances or based on a specific piece of news like a change in brokerage, an award, or a recognition. "Normally these would have been uncomfortable cold calls," says George. "But coming off the heels of a 'played video,' the call became warm."

To functionally eliminate cold calls, follow his lead. Introduce yourself through video, then follow up based on the reply or on the video play alert.

FIGURE 10.3 Example: Prospecting Video Email

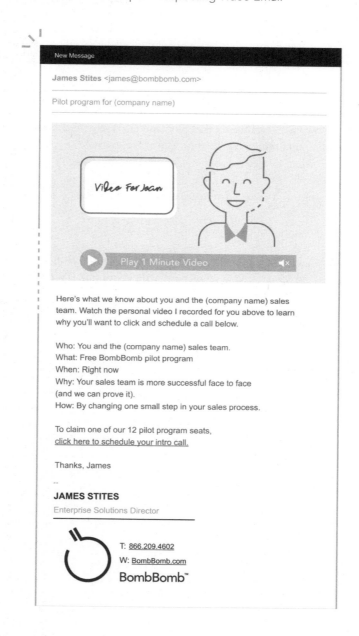

These tips for connecting with cold prospects are written toward video email, but you can apply them to social messaging if you've got that network connection or to text messaging if you've got her or his mobile number.

To increase opens, write your subject line like you're writing to a family member, friend, or coworker. Don't capitalize the first letter of every word. Use less formal and more casual language. Yes, you can use emojis if it's something you'd normally do. If you do use an emoji or two, try to make them relevant to the theme or message rather than simply being cute or fun. And whether it's emojis or some other approach, mix it up. Don't do the same thing every time.

Just as you want to make the subject line personal, the email itself should feel personal when your prospect opens it up. This means plain text instead of graphics-heavy HTML email designs. It also means concise, plain language rather than jargon-filled sales and marketing speak. Ideally (and sadly), it should be written to the 3rd grade level. When you do this, your video stands out more, especially if it's an animated preview that shows the person's name or another highly relevant detail.

Almost any system can mail merge or slug in a [First Name]. You might even be able to fake a name or highly relevant detail into a video thumbnail image or animated preview in front of an evergreen video. Tricking someone into thinking an evergreen video is personal, something that's easily discerned, probably isn't the best start to a relationship. It's like those fake handwritten notes. You know what can't be faked? Saying the person's name and speaking in specific detail when your recipient clicks play. This is the difference between personal and personalized. It's a difference people can feel. Showing each person that you took the time to do two minutes of research and record a truly personal 45-second video will dramatically improve your response rates.

A Personal Video to Every Prospect!?

You might be thinking, *I can't send a video to every prospect!* And you may be right. Your contact volume may be too high. But before you write it off completely, let's look at this idea through a segmenting exercise. If you send an email to 1,000 people and get a 25% open rate and 5% click rate, you'll get 12 or 13 people to wherever the click points. But if you sent a more targeted and, in theory, more relevant email to 250 people and get a 40% open rate and 12.5% click rate, you'll get the same number of people to the destination while annoying or negatively training many hundreds fewer people.

Now think about your quota, whether it's appointments set, appointments held, pipeline velocity, closed revenue, or another measure. Opens, clicks, and replies are all upstream. You can start with fewer people, but still exceed your goal simply by being more effective. Use your tracking, analytics, and alerts to follow up on your best opportunities in a truly personal way.

As is the case in so many aspects of our lives, the answer here is probably somewhere in between—some truly personal sends and some canned or automated sends. Do you have a half-dozen prospects named Charles who have two or three characteristics in common? Make the video email once and use it for all six (we're only partly kidding). On those canned or automated video emails, send based on triggers. For example, when these three criteria are met, send this video email to that person. You can speak to the trigger in such a way that the video truly feels personal; you can also add those details to your whiteboard note. We've both sent and received emails like this; they can be very effective. From there, pay attention to your analytics and use that information to follow up with the right people, in the right way, at the right time. For a model around this follow-up, turn to the next chapter.

CHAPTER 11

So, You Sent a Video . . . Now What?

You recorded a simple webcam or smartphone video and sent it to someone. Or you sent it to a list of people. Great! The more comfortable and familiar you get with this process, the more time you'll save by talking instead of typing. The more frequently your team connects with people personally, the more you'll accelerate sales and improve customer experience. Remember the OMG reply received by a software salesperson that we shared in the first chapter? No need to flip back, here it is again: "OMG that is the BEST email I have honestly EVER received! I mean no joke. It made me smile and I will give you any agenda you need! Wow! Totally made my day!"

That won't happen every time, but you can reasonably expect to receive more and warmer responses when you send personal videos in place of plain text. So, find your own top times to send video in emails, texts, and social. Figure out how video messages fit in with your phone calls, video conferences, text emails, and other communication. Start the practice and build the habit. And make the most of every second of video you record and every second of video that's watched.

In other words, have an answer to this question: So, you sent a video . . . now what?

What do you do if your email to one person doesn't get opened? What do you do if your video to a list of people only gets played by a few of them? What if your video email doesn't generate an immediate reply? We'll give you answers to all that and more. Adapt and apply these same tactics to your videos in text messaging or social messaging as needed.

HOW TRACKING HELPS YOU FOLLOW UP MORE EFFECTIVELY

You post a video, image, or a link on Facebook. They report 1,120 impressions. But your page has 18,705 fans. That's a 6% organic reach. Congratulations, you did better than average! But email would easily have reached four or five times more people. And you'd know *exactly* who each and every one of them was.

You upload a video to YouTube. They report 1,673 views. Nice. But who are the viewers and how can you follow up with them? Were 194 of the views from your Aunt Peggy and another 317 from the employee featured in the video? Or were they 1,673 unique individuals who represent legitimate opportunities to connect?

While we're at it, did anyone listen to those 64 voicemails you left yesterday? You'd have much better answers to these questions by mixing some video email into your outreach. So, pay attention to your tracking, analytics, and alerts. By knowing what a prospect, client, recruit, team member, supplier, or another stakeholder in your success did or didn't do with your video email, you're equipped with the information you need to follow up more effectively. You'll be better prepared to follow up at the right time and speak to what this person did or didn't see, experience, or do.

WHAT TO DO IF YOUR VIDEO EMAIL DIDN'T GET OPENED

To One Person

Have you given the person enough time to open it? The line between persistence and annoyance is thin. Give people 48 hours to take a look at it. And if you get an out-of-office reply, take note of the date of return. Even though most of us check our work email when we're out of the office, some people don't. Some systems will remind you to follow up on an unopened email or even resend it for you. For example, BombBomb allows you to set that reminder before sending, so it'll resurface the email in a day, a week, or whenever you want.

As for resending, that's your next step. But don't just send the exact same email again. Especially if you're sending into a cold situation, think through the elements that encourage people to open emails. Are your displayed name and email address consistent with each other and easily identifiable? Did you make clear in your subject line that something specific, useful, or interesting awaits inside? Is there another subject line you've used in a similar circumstance that was effective? Change up the subject line on a resend to reiterate the value or opportunity and resend it.

If your one-to-one video email didn't get opened, as in Figure 11.1, another option is to simply reply to the original video email and add a short line of text related to the value or opportunity; we'll detail this tactic in the discussion of what to do if your video doesn't get played.

To a List of People

For an average mass send, one in four or one in five people will open your email. For a well-segmented send, you might get to one in two or three people. If you've got a great subject line and great targeting, you might get to a 70% or 75% open rate, but that's as rare these days as a 10% organic reach with a Facebook post.

In a likelier scenario, more people will leave your mass email unopened than will open it. The first, most obvious question to ask in assessing who opened and who didn't is about how well targeted the email is. Did you send it to people who were unlikely to be interested? Did you just "blast" it out? Again, doing that for speed or from laziness is the fastest way to torch the value of the email addresses people have given you.

Assuming you did a reasonable job of sending your video email to people who would find it timely, relevant, and anticipated, further segment the original list down to people who didn't open the email. Any email system or CRM worth its subscription price should make this easy to do. Some will even do it automatically by allowing you to write workflow rules with if/then statements—*if* a person does this, *then* send this follow up, add her to this list, or tag her with this tag. In BombBomb, you can create new lists based

FIGURE 11.1 – If Your Video Email Didn't Get Opened

on action or non-action for email opens, link clicks, and video plays from the main email tracking screen. Your system should have a similar ability.

From here, you have the same two options as above, but we recommend only one. You can get away with a reply and the RE: with your original subject line in a personal send but using RE: and FWD: can feel a little spammy on a mass email. Instead, take the other recommendation. Create a new subject line that has more curiosity or more specificity related to the value inside the email, then resend it to your segmented lists of non-openers. Prior to doing this, we recommend waiting an extra day—72 hours or 3 days for a mass send, rather than 48 hours or 2 days on a personal send.

WHAT TO DO IF YOUR VIDEO DIDN'T GET PLAYED

To One Person

When you get started building trust and relationships through personal videos, you might feel shocked and disappointed that your play rate isn't 100%. You took the time to record it, so why wouldn't someone play it?! Feel free to linger in that moment, but don't wallow in it. (for simply "100% is perfection."). It's worth aspiring to, but you can't beat yourself up when you fall short. And you shouldn't quit the practice over it, either. Depending on how well you put together the elements shared in the previous chapter (targeting, subject line, email body, etc.), you might expect something more in the 50–75% range. But, again, experiencing you in person is an *extremely* high level of email engagement.

When you send a one-to-one video email that gets opened but that doesn't produce a video play, take a look at it. Did the subject line include the word "video" or make clear the value contained in the video? What did the static thumbnail image or animated preview of your video look like? Did you use a whiteboard or another device to make clear that it was truly personal and highly relevant? Or did you make a screen recording and start with something very specific and recognizable? Did you use a line or two of typed-out text above or below the video to further promise value and compel the click to play?

When someone understands that your video is truly one-to-one, it will stand out in his inbox and beg for a video play just like a handwritten note jumps out from all the junk mail in your traditional mailbox. The subject line, preview, and supporting text should work together to provide that understanding.

So, if your video doesn't get played, follow the steps for a non-open. Reply to the email and add a line or two of text reinforcing the reason you recorded and sent the video and reminding them of the opportunity (consider using the word "because" in asking for the play!). Or resend the email with a similar subject line, but better supporting text. An additional step is to go to the phone or another channel besides email. You know she knows you sent the video email, because she opened it. Leave a voicemail and refer to the video you sent and value it represents. Ask her to play the video and give you a call with a question about a *specific* detail or aspect of the video to create that curiosity gap, value assurance, and fear of missing out.

The video play should be closely linked in time to the email open, but consider giving another 12 to 24 hours after the original email open before reaching back out about the video play. A recipient may be excited about your video email, take a look at it during a meeting or appointment, but can't yet watch the video. This will result in an open, but no play. And you know how the day goes sometimes; even with the best intentions, he may forget to go back to it right away after getting tied up in other things after the meeting or appointment that prevented a video play concurrent with the email open. Let it sit. Be patient. Then follow up the next day if he's not played the video, as seen in Figure 11.2.

If you're open to adding another step to your process, you can run your video through a transcription app like Apple's Clips to add a text transcription over your video, so people can read along without having the sound on. Search the App Store or Google Play for something like "video transcription app" to

FIGURE 11.2 – If Your Video Didn't Get Played

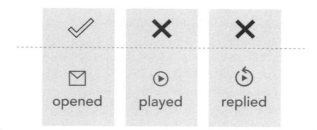

review options. If you go this route, be sure to include in the text that supports your video that people can watch with the sound off if they prefer. Obviously, this option is available to you when you send to a list of people, as well.

To a List of People

You might look at a 12% or 18% or even 24% video play rate on a mass email and think, *This doesn't work*. But it does. Click-through rates on mass emails are typically below 5%. And a video play is a much higher level of engagement. The people who clicked play experienced you in person. You created another trackable behavior. You helped drive the ultimate call to action with your very best and most persuasive asset . . . *you*! Your face, smile, expertise, enthusiasm, and all those qualities lost when you rely on text and static images to represent you. Still, as with email opens, you're not going to reach 100% on mass sends. And, as with email opens, it's difficult to get up over 50% except when it's extremely well targeted.

So, what do you do with the people who opened your email, but didn't play your video? Think about your video's relationship to the mass send. Was the video primarily a means to a separate, higher end? Or was the video an end in itself, the ultimate goal of the send? If it's a means to an end, your follow-up should be to focus on the broader opportunity, not on the video play. Segment the non-plays, then send another email or video email—or use a different communication channel.

If your mass video email has the video play as the desired outcome, segment the non-plays, then proceed with one of these two techniques (or blend them to create your own solution). First, you could duplicate then modify the original video email. Double-check the subject line. Strip out of the email body any friction or distraction from the video; everything should drive to the video play. Double-check the supporting text in the email body to make sure it's aligned with that goal. Then, send that updated email to your non-play segment.

As a second option, something we like to do that works really well is to send a completely new, lightweight email that links back to the original mass video email. This is like the inline reply to the unplayed video sent to one person but altered to accommodate mass sending. Most systems, whether an email marketing platform, a CRM, or another mass sending tool, should give you a link to your email. Get that link for the original video email you sent. Think of it as a click-through landing page for this new, text-only email. Promise the one or two most compelling or valuable things each person will get by playing the video. Write that into a short email and provide one clear link to your original video email. Consider using a subject line similar to your first send, because these people chose to open that original send. Make sure it's aligned with the value of the video, though, so that it works together with the contents of the email to deliver your desired outcome . . . more video plays.

WHAT TO DO IF YOU DIDN'T GET A REPLY

To One Person

This is a better scenario than the two others presented so far. Your email was delivered and opened, then your video was played. You know all this because you're paying attention to your analytics and alerts. This might be enough; you may only have wanted to convey information without making an additional ask. If, on the other hand, you asked for a reply or provided a call to action and your recipient didn't take you up on it, think about the answers to these questions. Did you ask them to do something not tracked in the inbox, like return a phone call or text message? If so, you've used video to help move the opportunity forward. If not, was your call to action clear? Did you make it obvious what the opportunity was and how to proceed? Did you even ask for a reply or another specific behavior? Any of these may be contributing factors.

Assuming you made clear the opportunity, knowing that you got the email open and video play lets you know that you've cleared the initial hurdles.

Follow up with a lightweight text email, a very short video, a phone call, or a text message. Don't say or write, "My video email system told me that you opened my email and played my video, so why haven't you responded?" Instead, try something like, "I sent you some information (about the topic). Did you receive it? Did you have any questions about it?"

Regardless of whether or not he or she has questions, you're likely to get a response just to confirm receipt. But you're also likely to get more information or context along with the confirmation. If your ask is conversational, you're almost certainly going to get something better than, "Yes, I got it." Like: "Yes, I got it, but . . ." or "Yes, I got it, and . . ." If you're using The Pro Method with a system equipped with a feature like BombBomb's Re/Actions, the opportunity to reply can be right there on the video, so it's an obvious and easy thing to do.[1]

Again, you can take the conversation out of the email chain or even offline completely if you don't get a reply, as captured conceptually in Figure 11.3. The purpose of the video is to get face to face to improve communication and build connection.

To a List of People

Replies to mass video emails are harder to come by than replies to truly personal sends. To increase them, start with the same line of inquiry as the previous list send scenario. The first and most obvious question: did you ask for a reply or make clear the call to action? Then: was the video play the end in itself or the means to another end? If your goal was the video view, no further follow-up is needed. If your goal was a reply, click, or another activity that some portion of your recipients didn't perform, reach back out to those people. Because they opened your email and played your video, you need to come with either a simple reminder or an entirely new angle. They may have intended to do it later and just need a reminder. Or they may have checked out your message in full but not seen or understood the value of saying, "Yes, I'll do that."

Across a large population, there's no way to know definitively which approach to take. Feedback from people who *did* take you up on your opportunity with a reply or a click may help you decide. Were there any frequently asked questions from people who've already said "yes" or replied with intent, but needed a question or two answered first? That may be the new angle you need to reposition the opportunity. No apparent friction from the "yes" group? The others may need a simple reminder with the urgency of a deadline.

FIGURE 11.3 If You Didn't Get a Reply or Response

MULTIPLE VIEWS, LATENT DEMAND, AND LONG-TERM FOLLOW-UP

A few common scenarios worth further exploration here include multiple views of a video sent only to one person or a small group, as experienced by Michael and the young family and by David and the dinner party back in Chapter 5. Another is recognizing opportunities that are easily missed for flying just under the radar. The third and final is using video to sustain connection over long or delayed sales and service cycles.

Multiple Views

A member of the CPAE Speaker Hall of Fame, Brad Montgomery uses professional videos or "marketing through video" on his website, in YouTube, and in other channels. These show what he's like as a performer on stage. But he also uses casual videos from his Denver office, sometimes wearing a ballcap or T-shirt, to land professional speaking gigs all over the world. These show what it's like to work with him as a person. You can see the difference in Figure 11.4. "Isn't it a cool irony that by making it simpler and cheaper and easier—boom!—it makes these videos even more effective?" asks Brad, who suggests using personal video "to get to the decision-makers who aren't talking to you on the phone. It's fantastic for this." Among the reasons he's sent more than 1,700 videos in three years' time: it gets him face to face with decision-makers even when there's a gatekeeper. Tracking lets him know he's succeeded, even in advance of the reply.

You'll get a similar story from Dallas-based musician and producer Ken Boome, who says that personal videos have "radically changed the way I do

FIGURE 11.4 Personal Videos Serve a Unique Purpose

 **versus**

business." Like Brad, Ken is often screened by an executive assistant or a committee member who represents one or more decision makers en route to getting the job. One of his best stories: "I sent the video to one person and about three minutes later, I'm getting analytics—boom, boom, boom. A half hour later, I have a signed contract and a deposit. That was a $1,200 gig." Could he have done that with a plain text email? Not likely. "She already feels like she knows me because the 'know, like, and trust' factor has been established with video," says Ken. Video puts you in front of decision-makers. Multiple views let you know that you made it behind the gate and pitched to those decision-makers "in person."

When you see multiple views racking up, anticipate a reply or a call. Or proactively reach out with some variation of, "I sent you some information. Did you receive it? Did you have any questions?" to prompt that reply or call. Multiple views on narrow sends most often mean you've been forwarded; it's affirmation that there's real interest from the person you sent it to.

Latent Demand

Being seen and heard doesn't just make you more persuasive, it also makes you more memorable. We remember more of what we see than what we hear. As we watch you in person or watch you on video, our mirror neurons mimic your behavior, sensations, and feelings; we share your experience.[2] This explains in part why sales is said to be the transfer of emotion. When you engage with someone through video, but it doesn't produce an immediate result, know that you'll likely be in the consideration set when it's time to make the decision because of the impression you left.

This manifests as an email open or video play alert on a video email you sent weeks, months, or even years ago. We see it all the time on our own sends. All within a 30-minute window, Richard opens up a newsletter from 19 months ago, an offer from 15 months ago, a personal video from 11 months ago, and a webinar follow-up from eight months ago. What's going on? He's going through his "BombBomb" folder where he filed away all those sends. But today's the day! He's finally ready to give it a real, in-depth look for himself and his team. What did I do when I saw those alerts come in? I gave his contact information to one of our Sales Development Reps, then sent a personal video thanking him for past interest and asking if he had any questions. Again, these analytics and cues to latent demand are what give email its incredible ROI.

In our previous consideration of responsive and unresponsive lead follow-up, we established that the decision timeline is different for different people. Making that initial, personal connection more memorable with video can keep you in consideration. Reinforce that by having lead nurturing habits or processes in place. That you're sending video in one of the easiest channels to track lets you know where there's latent demand in your database and tells you when to follow up.

Long-Term Follow-Up

We offered Richard a continuous flow of opportunities to participate with us. Live events, webinars, newsletters, special offers. What if you don't have these in place for your business? Or what if these things are the purview of the marketing department? In both cases, make it a habit to reach out with a video once per quarter or twice per year to people who represent open opportunities that aren't immediate.

You can do this on a one-to-one basis by making a habit to reach out to five or six people each morning a few mornings each week. The compounding effect of sending to six people three times per week puts you in front of nearly 900 people each year. And once you're comfortable, it's a 15- or 20-minute commitment per session—less than an hour per week! Your subject line, email body, and video preview should make clear you recorded the video just for her or him. They should either provide a specific promise of value or ask a simple question. Mention what you last talked about and create the opportunity to pick up where the conversation left off.

You can also do this on a one-to-many basis. Create the opportunity to experience you face to face in a channel that lets you know who's interested based on their actual behavior. Provide interesting or helpful information that relates to you, your brand, your product, or your service. Give an update on your industry or market. Use a screen recording to walk and talk through a timely topic. Your video doesn't have to be long or complex. It just needs to be you. If you pursue this path, use the analytics on the mass send to know who to reach on a one-to-one basis by video, phone, text, or another channel. In this way, you're prequalifying conversations.

NOW WHAT? THAT'S WHAT!

One of the main reasons email has the best return on investment among digital channels is that you know exactly who does what. You get specific feedback about people's actual behavior. Use it! Video email and video messaging are not silver bullets to cut through all your communication and conversion challenges. As you blend video into your business communication, use tracking to identify opportunities for more conversations and more conversions. Developing even simple processes for follow-up helps you make the most of your personal video practice.

CHAPTER 12

―――――

Where Rehumanization Is Now and Where It's Headed

The English word "education" has two different Latin roots: *educare* and *educere*. *Educare* means to train, to mold, or to nourish. *Educere* means to lead out, to draw from, or to bring forth.[1] Both have been goals leading into this final chapter. We've sought to share years of experience, insight, and expertise from pioneering the personal video movement with and through our customers and team members. That's *educare*. As the dozens of people mentioned in this book and thousands more like them have already done, you must reflect and self-identify as a participant and practitioner. You must discover your own motivations and find your opportunities to get started or to go deeper. That's *educere*. Our highest goal is to equip and inspire you to rehumanize some of your digital communication with personal video messages. You'll be glad you did. We need to see you.

The technologies, tools, and platforms described throughout this book will continue to change. Internet speeds will increase, as will smartphone and webcam video quality. Will our recorded, moving images become holographic? Will we blend virtual or augmented reality with recorded video images of ourselves in some hybrid medium? Will predictive analytics improve to the point that we know exactly who to send videos to every morning to reach the right people with the right message at the right time? Probably. But the opportunity that's in front of you right now is the opportunity you've had since you started working professionally. And it's the same opportunity you'll have as the technology changes.

Video's value is in *you*, not in the technology. Personal videos are about people, not about video. Video is simply the means to the end. It's a medium. A tool. The end is a stronger relationship with people than existed before you clicked "Record," "Stop," and "Send." Your opportunity is building trust and relationship with each person you work with to provide value and generate revenue.

What's happening is less a revolution and more a pendulum swing back from our over-reliance on typed-out text, automations, and other faceless, digital communication. We're moving back toward a more personal and human approach. This is why we call it rehumanizing, rather than humanizing. Video gives you a new/old way to sell and serve. It's a return to the way business was done for generations . . . face to face.

Since we started on this journey back in 2006, many people have completely missed this point. They see personal video as a technology play, sales gimmick, faddish novelty, or parlor trick. These are the people who send one or two videos, expect magic to happen, and quit when it doesn't. They're the people who see sales exclusively as manipulation rather than an equitable exchange of value. They're the people who see a potential customer for his or her transactional value, not as the source of 10 more customers.

Because you picked up this book in the first place and got this far, we expect you're not among them. Instead, you see the value of taking a warmer approach to leadership, sales, customer service, recruiting, teamwork, and all the other roles and functions you find yourself in that require better communication and trusting relationships. You see this as a way of being, not just something you're trying or doing. Or you at least see its promise.

MORE EFFECTIVE AND MORE SATISFYING WORK

In the opening chapter, you saw data collected from approximately 500 people comparing video email to traditional email. They reported more replies, more clicks, higher conversion, more referrals, and a greater ability to stay in touch. These are all great outcomes. They're compelling reasons to get going with video if you've not yet started or to double down if you've only dabbled. But the true value of this approach to business communication has not yet been established, even though most of us know it intuitively. That value is in human connection.

Remember Andrew Brodsky, PhD, the assistant professor at the McCombs School of Business at the University of Texas at Austin? We introduced him in Chapter 2. Andrew's research is primarily in organizational behavior and communication. As a doctoral candidate, he led a research project with a team at Harvard Business School exploring the dynamics of traditional email and video email within our community. While trying to come up with the right design to get at the themes he wanted to explore in the study, Andrew decided it would be useful to interview several of our customers. I sought the permission of several of our most prolific video users, then shared their contact information with him.

After he conducted several interviews, Andrew reported back some of his findings. He heard from the video users something we'd prepared him for: that the people you send videos to feel like they know you before they ever meet you and that the results achieved by getting face to face are better than results achieved by sending plain text. But Andrew also heard something from our customers that we'd not ever heard ourselves: that sending videos doesn't just make the recipient feel closer to the sender, it also makes the sender feel closer to the recipient. Of course!

Of course the dynamic goes both ways. Relationships go both ways. Connection is between two people. So even though it's an asynchronous, one-way medium, personal video isn't just a more effective way to work, it's also a more satisfying way to work. We're not just better face to face, we *thrive* face to face. Our highest purpose is to be in relationship with other people. One of our deepest needs is to connect with others. This qualitative feedback did not get tested or quantified in the study, but it's deeply interesting and important to us as we continue to explore and advance rehumanization with video.

We don't know how common this phenomenon is or how it works. We're not sure what it is about the practice that draws us closer to our recipients. We're not clear on why we're psychologically or emotionally drawn closer to people, even when we can't see them. We expect it's tied to soft-sounding concepts like vulnerability and authenticity. You're showing people who you really are. You're opening up, letting your guard down, and being honest with them. There's a vulnerability there and a fear of judgment, rejection, and shame. The honesty in truly *being* with someone in person or in video builds trust, which is the foundation of any satisfying relationship.

As we shared in the opening of Chapter 3, satisfying relationships are the greatest predictor of human health and well being. This finding was reinforced by research drawing on data from four longitudinal studies like The Grant Study. A team at the University of North Carolina at Chapel Hill blended social and biological perspectives and found that social isolation in teens creates the same risk of inflammation as not exercising. In older adults, social isolation creates the same risk of developing hypertension as having diabetes. Our social connections "get under our skin" and affect us physically. These researchers sought to understand how and why. The recommendation of one of the study's authors: "Do have a good and healthy diet, and exercise; but also try to have a good social life and connections with other people. Cultivate broad and somewhat deep, functional [relationships]. That's as important, if not more—and don't wait until you're old."[2]

If this is starting to feel soft to you, that's in part the point. There's a dynamic at play that we'll continue to explore with the customers and community growing around personal videos. To give another set of language to the more effective/more satisfying dynamic, we'll look to the publisher of *Forbes* . . .

THE SOFT EDGE

"There have never been more ways to reach consumers than there are today. That's a fact. But it's also never been harder to connect deeply with consumers," writes *Forbes* publisher Rich Karlgaard in his book *The Soft Edge: Where Great Companies Find Lasting Success*.[3] He goes on to establish that customer relationships are necessary precursors to transactions and valuable foundations for future repeat and referral business. Echoing Seth Godin in *Permission Marketing*, Karlgaard wraps in the escalation of relationship from prospect to customer to friend to fan. Deep connection is the key and video can help.

The premise of Karlgaard's book is that hard-edge skills like speed, cost, supply chain, logistics, and capital efficiency unfairly overshadow soft edge skills like trust, smarts, teamwork, story, and design. In his triangular model, hard and soft skills are equal sides built upon a strategic base of markets, customers, competitors, substitutes, and disrupters. In business, we tend to focus on what's easy to measure. It gives us a sense of control and accomplishment. As a result, the more easily measured hard edge gets more attention than the equally important soft edge.

In customer success, the hard edge is captured in ticket volume, first reply time, time to resolution, call counts, and call times. But the soft edge qualities of connection, satisfaction, and word-of-mouth affect all the hard-edge measures.

In inside sales, the hard edge is captured in appointments held, call counts, email counts, close rates, transaction value, pace to goal, and revenue. But the soft edge qualities of trust, rapport, storytelling, discovery, diagnosis, and prescription impact all the hard-edge measures.

With personal video in email, the hard edge is captured in reply rates, click rates, and conversion rates. But the soft edge qualities of trust, teamwork, and story are also in play. You understand intuitively that relationships matter, even though they're soft edge.

As you weigh the opportunity laid out over the course of these pages, don't lose sight of the inherent benefits of rehumanizing your communication and your business just because some of them can't yet be measured. Participating in this movement will require building new skills and new habits. Many have quit before they ever really got started. But the movement won't be stopped.

THE STATE OF THE MOVEMENT

With all this in mind, know that this movement is still very young. A few hundred thousand or perhaps half a million people are actively participating right now. But there are 60.6 million people working in a professional or managerial capacity in the United States alone.[4] And 5.7 million Americans working in formal sales roles.[5] Expand these numbers globally and you're immediately at hundreds of millions, with billions of potential practitioners behind them. Remember Daniel Pink's thesis in *To Sell Is Human*? Every working professional teaches, trains, or sells. If they don't sell products or services directly, they sell ideas and opportunities. They connect, influence, and persuade. They're each in the change business. And video helps them do all these things the way these things have been done best since our species has stood erect on two feet: face to face.

More people are participating every day, which creates a pull. But there's also a push behind this. Venture-backed, video-based companies that began with a focus on scripted, lit, produced, and edited marketing videos are uprooting and unmooring to move "down market" toward this simpler style. New startups are instantly adopting the language of trust, relationship, and humanization to try to get traction for me-too video tools. Every social network has been building and expanding video features for years now, including in their messaging toolsets.

On the hardware side, cameras remain a key battleground for smartphone manufacturers, as our phones have become the most popular camera system.[6] The webcam market is projected to grow to $15.2B by 2021, more than quadruple its $3.4B in 2014.[7] Sales revenue of Canon, a traditional camera, imaging, and camcorder manufacturer, peaked in 2007.[8] Action camera leader GoPro's revenue peaked in 2015.[9] Professional video and high-end equipment are still incredibly useful, but the trend favors simpler video.

As new, novel, or uncomfortable as your first 10 webcam or smartphone videos may feel, you're getting ahead of the curve. If you're in a competitive environment, then differentiating yourself and proving you work differently provides an immediate win. Even if you're not in a competitive environment, you're building trust, accelerating sales, and improving experience. You're reducing email reply chains or back-and-forth phone calls by being clear and complete in video messages. You're laying the groundwork for an internal culture that prefers to get face to face with all its stakeholders more often. We've seen entire sales teams build each other up and transition to a video-first culture together. We've seen internal communication improve organizational connection and engagement, especially across distributed locations and remote workers. This is all part of the personal video opportunity.

And if you're wondering about the effects of ages and generations on video recording and sending, our current customers run the full range of the workforce, from young 20-somethings through people beyond retirement age who continue to work because they find it fulfilling. Some use it to connect with younger consumers. Others report that their most favorable responses come from their older clients. Ultimately, as a new/old way to sell and serve, this is about people connecting with people, not about specific ages or generations. If you have something valuable to share with another person and video is a good medium for that message, the different ages of you and your recipient are not especially relevant.

On the sending side and consistent with broader cultural trends, younger people seem to be more comfortable appearing in photos and videos. But millennials also tend to strive for perfection, more so than previous generations, according to a study by the American Psychological Association.[10] Depression and anxiety are the result of heightened self-expectations and desire for control. The image-based nature of Instagram, Snapchat, and Facebook is deeply intertwined in this problem.

"Social media drives this pressure to present the coolest version of themselves, otherwise known as the 'Instagram effect' . . . Teens will openly admit to taking countless photos in an attempt to get the best shot," write Jeff Fromm and Angela Read in their book *Marketing to Gen Z*, whom they call the Pivotal generation.[11] Because of this, younger people may struggle with getting comfortable on camera, just as everyone else does.

But this generation does prefer that *you* get comfortable on camera. "Because clever marketing tricks and gimmicks don't fool Pivotals, building authentic relationships with them is key," Fromm and Read write. These younger consumers and workers expect personalized messages, as well as honesty, empathy, and even friendship. We all crave relationships and authenticity; as technology evolves and proliferates, our deep need for human connection remains. It makes sense, then, that digital natives crave authenticity as much or more than older generations.

By getting started, building new skills, and creating new habits today, you're setting yourself up for a more effective and more satisfying work experience for years to come. If you're 20 years or more into your career, you may not recognize how much you know about connecting, communicating, and converting. It's time to transfer the experience and expertise you may be taking for granted into a medium that puts you in an even better position to succeed. Before it becomes more common and before more consumers demand it. Though you may struggle to get confident on camera, you've got a wealth of knowledge, expertise, and insights to offer. And you'll do it better in video.

If you're just getting started or just coming up in your career, you'll find that a more personal approach starts more conversations and opens more doors, especially if it's got curiosity and sincerity woven in. Don't shoot for perfection. Don't re-record. Just be yourself.

MEASURING MORE THAN OPENS, PLAYS, AND REPLIES

In our view, the tracking and analytics behind this video movement remain as nascent as the movement itself. As we've established, tracking provides significant value to you as you record, send, and follow up. You need to know who's opening your emails, when someone is playing your video, and how often you receive replies. But there's so much further to go in discovering what's really working best and following its evolution over the years to come. When Andrew Brodsky engaged us as a doctoral candidate at Harvard Business School, part of his interest was in the dearth of research in this area of business communication. We've got much to learn.

Each and every video itself is full of data that have not yet been unpacked. For example, how do the following factors affect play rates, play to completion rates, reply rates, and other measures?

- Video length of different types of videos
- Pace of speech
- Number, duration, and timing of pauses
- Specific words or phrases spoken
- Frequency and duration of smiles
- Frequency and duration of eye contact
- Range of facial expressions of emotion
- Framing and size of the subject's head and shoulders
- Ability to see hands and hand gestures
- Frequency and range of hand gestures
- Placement of face during screen recording
- Recording inside versus recording outside
- Recording in a cubicle versus an office versus a common area
- Recording while seated versus while standing
- Gender and age of the subject versus gender and age of recipient(s)
- Formality of the subject's attire
- Number of speakers in the video
- Frequency of video sends to a specific recipient

Measuring these factors and their effects across millions of videos in real time requires that we build and train systems to read them properly. Twice during a BombBomb Hack Week, when our software development team members work on whatever they want, developers have taken on facial recognition, smiles, emotion, gender, age, and other qualities. We've not yet moved this work beyond experimentation. They're neither widely deployed, nor functionally applicable to your day-to-day video use. But the potential is there.

The goal is to move beyond "Here's what happened" and a bit of "Here's what to do about it" to deeper prescription by specific use case. Imagine: when you need to apologize, here are five specific recommendations for your pace, tone, and body language—and a couple of phrases you might want to use, as well as one you'll definitely want to avoid. As more people put this video philosophy into practice, more attention and resources will be paid by organizations of all kinds—from business to academia—to the data available in a growing sample of videos.

YOUR NEXT STEPS

Yesterday was the best day to start replacing some of your text-based messages with personal videos. Today is the next best day to get in the practice, to get comfortable and confident, to get early wins, and to get ahead of the curve. Rehumanizing your business is more effective and more satisfying for you, your team members, and your customers.

Next Steps as an Individual Practitioner

If you're an individual practitioner, start by listing some of your best opportunities to add video for better results. Think about the stories and examples shared in Chapter 5, "Nine Stories of Sales Acceleration and Better Customer Experience," and throughout this book. Think about the situations described and illustrated in Chapter 6, "Ten Times to Send Video Instead of Plain, Typed-Out Text." Identify one or two specific videos or use cases to start with—such as thank-you, great to meet you, or happy birthday messages. Identify two or three more to grow into—such as lead follow-up, nurturing, and conversion or checking in with people in your network.

Then, evaluate your current toolset. What software and systems do you currently use for email, for sales and marketing features, for customer relationship management, and other uses? Which do you intend to keep? Which might you drop? Where does video fit into any of those systems or tools? Do any video or video email providers that deliver The Pro Method defined in

Chapter 7 connect directly with or work within your systems, such as Gmail, Outlook, iOS, or Android? Or do they connect to other systems you use through middleware like Zapier?

Be clear about your needs, wants, and current situation as you focus on the best ways to get started building relationships through video. Don't let equipment or experience be excuses not to move forward. Start with what you have and know that you'll get better and better as you go forward. You'll find new and interesting opportunities to use video. You'll get replies and responses that you're not getting now. You'll communicate more clearly, connect more effectively, and convert at a higher rate. And you'll likely have fun doing it.

If you need any help along the way, review the stories and tips provided here in this book. And visit the companion website for even more stories and tips.

Visit BombBomb.com/BookBonus to get stories, tips, and examples.

Next Steps as a Team, Department, or Company

Whether you're on a sales team, customer success team, talent management team, leadership team, or another type of team, the ideas shared for individual practitioners apply to you. But think about it for you *and* your team members. The use cases and stories you found most applicable in this book give you a great starting point for the best ways to start with video. What are the key metrics you're trying to move? For sales, is it appointments set? Appointments held? Total conversion rate? For customer success, is it customer satisfaction? Time to resolution? Ticket volume handled per person?

Think about the numbers you're trying to move. Would a more personal touch and higher quality communication make an impact? Where in your process should you add a truly personal video? Should it be before or after a phone call? Where in your processes can you add a pre-recorded, evergreen video? Should each team member make her or his own? If you've not outlined your communication cadences and flows, now might be a good time to do that. Or it could be as simple as: let's keep doing what we're doing but add a personal video here and add an evergreen video there.

You'll also want to evaluate your tech stack. Video needs to be accessible within or immediately adjacent to the software systems and platforms you're using right now. Are you using Gmail or Outlook? Or Salesforce? Or Zendesk? Identify the main places you're sending outbound messages to the people who matter most to your business. Then look for scaled Pro Method solutions that match up.

Try out your best-fit video solutions as an individual or as a pilot for your entire team. Then use it during that trial period! There's nothing worse than committing, but not committing fully. Don't let your trial experience end without real use and evaluation. Did your theories about best use cases to move your KPIs hold true? Did you identify new opportunities for your team to use video? Who used it the most or the best? What can you teach others based on what your top performers did? What was overall adoption? How will you increase that when the solution is more formally implemented?

Look for a partner who can help you ask questions like these, find great answers to those questions, and work within your current systems. For team-oriented tips and assets, reach out to us or visit the companion site.

Visit BombBomb.com/BookBonus to get team-oriented tips and assets.

REHUMANIZE YOUR COMMUNICATION AND YOUR BUSINESS

The foundation is laid. The opportunity is clear. The time is now. Stop hiding behind plain, typed-out text and start getting face to face with more people more often. Encourage and equip your team to do the same. To build trust, relationships, and success with greater speed and satisfaction, add some video to your day-to-day communication. Because we need and want to see you. And because you'll love the results.

NOTES

Chapter 1 The New Way to Communicate, Connect, and Convert

1. Beute, Ethan. "Survey: 77% of People Benefit from Video Email, 20% Double Results." BombBomb. October 2, 2015. https://bombbomb.com/blog/video-email-survey-results-reply-response-referral/.
2. Beute, Ethan. "New Data: 78.8% of People Improve Gmail Results with BombBomb." BombBomb. July 27, 2017. https://bombbomb.com/blog/gmail-results-improve-video-email-data-survey/.
3. Mehrabian, Albert. *Silent Messages*, Vol. 8 (Belmont, CA: Wadsworth, 1971): 77.
4. Schroeder, Juliana, and Epley, Nicholas. "Speaking Louder Than Words: Voice Reveals the Presence of a Humanlike Mind." Unpublished manuscript, University of Chicago (2014).

Chapter 2 Email: The Indispensable, Broken Tool

1. Backman, Maurie. "How Much Time Are You Wasting on Work Emails?" *The Motley Fool*. September 21, 2017. https://www.fool.com/careers/2017/09/21/how-much-time-are-you-wasting-on-work-emails.aspx.
2. Dubé, Dani-Elle. "This Is How Much Time You Spend On Work Emails Every Day, According to a Canadian Survey." *Global News*. April 21, 2017. https://globalnews.ca/news/3395457/this-is-how-much-time-you-spend-on-work-emails-every-day-according-to-a-canadian-survey/.
3. "2018 Adobe Consumer Email Survey." Adobe Systems Incorporated. August 17, 2018. https://www.slideshare.net/adobe/2018-adobe-consumer-email-survey.
4. Ibid.
5. Bauer, Emily. "15 Outrageous Email Spam Statistics That Still Ring True in 2018." Propeller. February 1, 2018. https://www.propellercrm.com/blog/email-spam-statistics.
6. "15 Text Messaging Statistics Every Business Should Know." Intelligent Contacts, Inc. Accessed August 27, 2018. https://intelligentcontacts.com/15-text-messaging-statistics-every-business-should-know/.
7. Madrigal, Alexis. "Why No One Answers Their Phone Anymore." *The Atlantic*. May 31, 2018. https://www.theatlantic.com/technology/archive/2018/05/ring-ring-ring-ring/561545/.
8. Crother, Brooke. "Nearly Half All Cell Phone Calls Will Be Scams by 2019, Report Says." Fox News Network, LLC. September 21, 2018. https://www.foxnews.com/tech/nearly-half-all-cell-phone-calls-will-be-scams-by-2019-report-says.
9. Email Statistics Report, 2018–2022. London: The Radicati Group, Inc., 2018. Accessed August 27, 2018. https://www.radicati.com/wp/wp-content/uploads/2018/01/Email_Statistics_Report,_2018–2022_Executive_Summary.pdf.

10. "Email Continues to Deliver Strong ROI and Value for Marketers." *eMarketer.* September 12, 2016. https://www.emarketer.com/Article/Email-Continues-Deliver-Strong-ROI-Value-Marketers/1014461.

11. "2018 Email Marketing Industry Census." *eConsultancy of Centaur Media.* June 2018. https://econsultancy.com/reports/email-census/.

12. "The Ultimate List of Marketing Statistics for 2018." HubSpot. Accessed August 28, 2018. https://www.hubspot.com/marketing-statistics.

13. Roesler, Peter. "Study Shows Email Marketing Still Popular and Effective with Millennials." *Inc.* March 28, 2016. Accessed August 30, 2018. https://www.inc.com/peter-roesler/study-shows-email-marketing-still-popular-and-effective-with-millennials.html.

14. Brodsky, Andrew. 2018. "Chapter 3: Overcrafting of Business Correspondence: The Effectiveness, Productivity, and Affective Consequences of Impression Management in text-based communication." PhD diss., Harvard University.

15. Kruger, Justin, Epley, Nicholas, Parker, Jason, and Ng, Zhi-Wen. "Egocentrism Over E-mail: Can We Communicate As Well As We Think?" *Journal of Personality and Social Psychology 89*, no. 6 (2005): 925.

16. Schroeder, Juliana, and Epley, Nicholas. "Speaking Louder Than Words: Voice Reveals the Presence of a Humanlike Mind." Unpublished manuscript, University of Chicago (2014).

17. Marche, Stephen. "The Epidemic of Facelessness." *The New York Times*, February 14, 2015. Accessed September 5, 2018. https://www.nytimes.com/2015/02/15/opinion/sunday/the-epidemic-of-facelessness.html.

18. Miller, Hannah, Thebault-Spieker, Jacob, Chang, Shuo, Johnson, Isaac, Terveen, Loren, and Hecht, Brent. "'Blissfully Happy' or 'Ready to Fight': Varying Interpretations of Emoji." Proceedings of ICWSM 2016 (2016).

Chapter 3 Video: The Personal, Rehumanizing Tool

1. Mineo, Liz. "Good Genes Are Nice, but Joy Is Better." *The Harvard Gazette.* April 11, 2017. https://news.harvard.edu/gazette/story/2017/04/over-nearly-80-years-harvard-study-has-been-showing-how-to-live-a-healthy-and-happy-life/.

2. Vaynerchuk, Gary. *The Thank You Economy* (New York: Harper Business, 2011): 3.

3. Burg, Bob, and Mann, John David. *The Go-Giver* (New York: Portfolio, 2007): 82.

4. King, Barbara. "When Did Human Speech Evolve?" NPR. September 5, 2013. https://www.npr.org/sections/13.7/2013/09/05/219236801/when-did-human-speech-evolve.

5. Hammer, Joshua. "Finally, the Beauty of France's Chauvet Cave Makes its Grand Public Debut." *Smithsonian Magazine.* April 2015. https://www.smithsonianmag.com/history/france-chauvet-cave-makes-grand-debut-180954582/.

6. Neuendorf, Henri. "Turkish Archaeologists Discover the World's Oldest Known Writings." artnet news. July 2015. https://news.artnet.com/art-world/turkey-worlds-oldest-writing-pictograph-319107.

7. Mark, Joshua J. "Cuneiform." *Ancient History Encyclopedia.* Last modified March 15, 2018. https://www.ancient.eu/cuneiform/.

8. Roser, Max, and Ortiz-Ospina, Estaban. "Literacy." OurWorldInData.org. Last modified September 20, 2018. https://ourworldindata.org/literacy.

9. Stanislas, Dehaene, Pegado, Felipe, Braga, Lucia W., Ventura, Paulo, Filho, Gilberto Nunes, Jobert, Antoinette, Dehaene-Lambertz, Ghislaine, Kolinsky, Régine, Morais, José, and Cohen, Laurent. "How Learning to Read Changes the Cortical Networks for Vision and Language." *Science* (2010): 1194140.

10. Matsumoto, David, Frank, Mark G., and Hwang, Hyi Sung, eds. *Nonverbal Communication: Science and Applications* (Newbury Park, CA: Sage, 2013): 16, 55.

11. McClure, Max. "Infants Process Faces Long Before They Recognize Other Objects, Stanford Vision Researchers Find." *Stanford Report.* December 11, 2012. https://news.stanford.edu/news/2012/december/infants-process-faces-121112.html.

12. Bergland, Christopher. "The Neuroscience of Making Eye Contact." *Psychology Today.* March 25, 2014. https://www.psychologytoday.com/us/blog/the-athletes-way/201403/the-neuroscience-making-eye-contact.

13. Lavine, Robert. "The Hormones and Brain Regions Behind Eye Contact." *The Scientist.* August 1, 2016. https://www.the-scientist.com/notebook/the-hormones-and-brain-regions-behind-eye-contact-33100.

14. Jarrett, Christian. "Why It's Hard to Talk and Make Eye Contact at the Same Time." *Research Digest.* November 18, 2016. https://digest.bps.org.uk/2016/11/18/why-its-hard-to-talk-and-make-eye-contact-at-the-same-time/.

15. Mason, Malia, Hood, Bruce, and Macrae, C. Neil. "Look into My Eyes: Gaze Direction and Person Memory." *Memory 12*, no. 5 (2004): 637–643.

16. Kreysa, Helene, Kessler, Luise, and Schweinberger, Stefan R. "Direct Speaker Gaze Promotes Trust in Truth-Ambiguous Statements." *PloS ONE 11*, no. 9 (2016): e0162291.

17. Iizuka, Yuichi. "Evaluation of Gaze Pairs by Female Observers." *The Japanese Journal of Experimental Social Psychology 31*, no. 3 (1992): 231–239.

18. Larsen, Randy J., and Shackelford, Todd K. "Gaze Avoidance: Personality and Social Judgments of People Who Avoid Direct Face-to-Face Contact." *Personality and individual Differences 21*, no. 6 (1996): 907–917.

19. Bergo, Bettina, "Emmanuel Levinas." *The Stanford Encyclopedia of Philosophy* (Fall 2017 Edition), Edward N. Zalta (ed.). https://plato.stanford.edu/archives/fall2017/entries/levinas/.

20. Wang, Yin, Ramsey, Richard, and Hamilton, Antonia. "The Control of Mimicry by Eye Contact Is Mediated by Medial Prefrontal Cortex." *Journal of Neuroscience 31*, no. 33 (2011): 12001–12010.

21. "20 Hand Gestures You Should Be Using." *Science of People.* Accessed September 5, 2018. https://www.scienceofpeople.com/hand-gestures/.

22. Gregoire, Carolyn. "The Fascinating Science behind 'Talking' with Your Hands." *The Huffington Post.* February 4, 2016. https://www.huffingtonpost.com/entry/talking-with-hands-gestures_us_56afcfaae4b0b8d7c230414e.

23. Weinschenk, Susan. "Your Hand Gestures Are Speaking for You." *Psychology Today.* September 26, 2012. https://www.psychologytoday.com/us/blog/brain-wise/201209/your-hand-gestures-are-speaking-you.

24. Beute, Ethan. "Benefits of a Smile in Video and in Sales." *BombBomb*. December 18, 2014. https://bombbomb.com/blog/benefits-smile-video-sales/.

25. Kahneman, Daniel, and Patrick Egan. *Thinking, Fast and Slow*. Vol. 1 (New York: Farrar, Straus and Giroux): 2011.

26. Clark, Brian. "Click, Whirr, Buy." *Copyblogger*. February 21, 2006. https://www.copyblogger.com/click-whirr-buy/.

27. Matsumoto, Frank, and Hwang, *Nonverbal Communication*.

Chapter 4 Six Signs This New Approach Is for You and Your Business

1. Pink, Daniel H. *To Sell Is Human: The Surprising Truth about Moving Others* (London: Penguin, 2013): 21.

2. Daugherty, Paul, and Wilson, H. James. *Human + Machine: Reimagining Work in the Age of AI* (Boston: Harvard Business Review Press, 2018): 92.

3. Roghanizad, M. Mahdi, and Bohns, Vanessa K. "Ask in Person: You're Less Persuasive Than You Think over Email." *Journal of Experimental Social Psychology 69* (2017): 223–226.

Chapter 5 Nine Stories of Sales Acceleration and Better Customer Experience

1. Pink, Daniel H. *To Sell Is Human: The Surprising Truth About Moving Others* (London: Penguin, 2013): 1, 178.

2. Carmody, Dennis P., and Lewis, Michael. "Brain Activation When Hearing One's Own and Others' Names." *Brain Research 1116*, no. 1 (2006): 153–158.

3. Williams, Lisa A., and Bartlett, Monica Y. "Warm Thanks: Gratitude Expression Facilitates Social Affiliation in New Relationships via Perceived Warmth." *Emotion 15*, no. 1 (2015): 1.

Chapter 6 Ten Times to Use Video Instead of Plain, Typed-Out Text

1. Whitbourne, Susan Krauss. "5 Ways to Deliver Bad News With a Minimum of Pain." *Psychology Today*. July 25, 2015. https://www.psychologytoday.com/us/blog/fulfillment-any-age/201507/5-ways-deliver-bad-news-minimum-pain.

2. Heskett, James L., and Sasser, W. Earl. "The Service Profit Chain." In *Handbook of Service Science* (Boston: Springer, 2010): 19–29.

3. Solomon, Lou. "The Top Complaints from Employees About Their Leaders." *Harvard Business Review*. June 24, 2015. https://hbr.org/2015/06/the-top-complaints-from-employees-about-their-leaders.

4. "2018 Adobe Consumer Email Survey." Adobe Systems Incorporated. August 17, 2018. https://www.slideshare.net/adobe/2018-adobe-consumer-email-survey.

Chapter 7 Sending Video in Emails, Text Messages, and Social Messages

1. "Email Client Market Share." Litmus. Accessed September 25, 2018. http://emailclientmarketshare.com/.

Chapter 8 Why You're Not Sending Video and How to Get Comfortable on Camera

1. Browne, Brené. "The Power of Vulnerability." Filmed June 2010 in in Houston, TX. TED Video, 20:13. https://www.ted.com/talks/brene_brown_on_vulnerability?language=en.
2. Reynolds, Susan. "Happy Brain, Happy Life." *Psychology Today*, August 2, 2011. https://www.psychologytoday.com/us/blog/prime-your-gray-cells/201108/happy-brain-happy-life.

Chapter 9 The Salesperson's Guide to Video Cameras

1. Gamez, Victor. "Visual Realism: The Way to Build Trust with Your Audience." Content Marketing Institute. February 19, 2016. https://contentmarketinginstitute.com/2016/02/visual-realism-trust/.

Chapter 10 How to Get More Opens, Plays, and Replies

1. Williams, Robert. "Study: Email Marketing Revenue Hits Record Growth." *Mobile Marketer*. June 22, 2017. https://www.mobilemarketer.com/news/study-email-marketing-revenue-hits-record-growth/445565/.
2. Forer, Laura. Email Optimization: Case Studies and Actionable Tips [Infographic]. September 27, 2018. https://i.marketingprofs.com/assets/images/daily-chirp/180927-infographic-email-marketing-optimization-hacks-full.jpg.
3. Waldow, D. J., and Falls, Jason. *The Rebel's Guide to Email Marketing: Grow Your List, Break the Rules, and Win* (Indianapolis: Que Publishing, 2012).
4. Beute, Ethan. "Test Results: Animated GIF Delivers 48.9% Lift in Video Play Rate." BombBomb. April 7, 2016. https://bombbomb.com/blog/animated-gif-video-play-rate-test-results/.
5. "Principles of Persuasion." Influence at Work. Accessed September 28, 2018. https://www.influenceatwork.com/principles-of-persuasion/.
6. Weinschenk, Susan. "The Power of the Word 'Because' to Get People to Do Stuff." *Psychology Today*. October 15, 2013. https://www.psychologytoday.com/us/blog/brain-wise/201310/the-power-the-word-because-get-people-do-stuff.

Chapter 11 So, You Sent a Video . . . Now What?

1. Menor, Alli. "Increase Your Sales Email Response Rate with Re/Actions by BombBomb." BombBomb. October 9, 2018. https://bombbomb.com/blog/increase-your-sales-email-response-rate-with-re-actions-by-bombbomb/.

2. Kinsey Goman, Carol. "Why You Are More Successful in Face-To-Face Meetings." *Forbes*. October 25, 2015. https://www.forbes.com/sites/carolkinseygoman/2015/10/25/why-you-are-more-successful-in-face-to-face-meetings/#14c5c7cd6315.

Chapter 12 Where Rehumanization Is Now and Where It's Headed

1. Bass, Randall V., and Good, J. W. "Educare and Educere: Is a Balance Possible in the Educational System?" *The Educational Forum 68*, no. 2 (2004): 161–168.
2. Izadi, Elahe. "Your Relationships Are Just As Important to Your Health As Diet and Exercise." *The Washington Post*. January 5, 2016. https://www.washingtonpost.com/news/to-your-health/wp/2016/01/05/your-relationships-are-just-as-important-to-your-health-as-exercising-and-eating-well/?utm_term=.97479e992bfd.
3. Karlgaard, Rich. *The Soft Edge: Where Great Companies Find Lasting Success* (Hoboken, NJ: John Wiley & Sons, 2014): 183.
4. "Distribution of Nonelderly Adult Workers by Occupational Category." Kaiser Family Foundation. Accessed July 30, 2018. https://www.kff.org/other/state-indicator/blue-and-white-collar-workers/?dataView=1&currentTimeframe=0&sortModel=%7B%22colId%22:%22Professionals%20%26%20Managers%22,%22sort%22:%22desc%22%7D#notes.
5. Krogue, Ken. "New Sales Trend Research: US Sales Reps Lagging behind European Counterparts." *Forbes*. September 26, 2017. https://www.forbes.com/sites/kenkrogue/2017/09/26/new-sales-trend-research-us-sales-reps-lagging-behind-european-counterparts/#5ef5624f632f.
6. "Distribution of Camera System Sales Worldwide in 2012 and 2016, by Type Of Camera." Statista. Accessed October 1, 2018. https://www.statista.com/statistics/282074/distribution-camera-system-sales-worldwide/.
7. "WebCam Market Is Expected to Grow $15.2 Billion by 2021." Radiant Insights, Inc. Accessed October 1, 2018. https://globenewswire.com/news-release/2015/08/17/761212/10146240/en/WebCam-Market-Is-Expected-To-Grow-15–2-Billion-By-2021-Radiant-Insights-Inc.html.
8. "Canon's Net Sales Worldwide from 2006 to 2017 (in Billion Yen)." Statista. Accessed October 1, 2018. https://www.statista.com/statistics/236434/total-revenue-of-canon/.
9. "MarketWatch: GoPro Inc." MarketWatch. Accessed October 1, 2018. https://www.marketwatch.com/investing/stock/gpro/financials.
10. Curran, Thomas, and Hill, Andrew P. "Perfectionism Is Increasing over Time: A Meta-Analysis of Birth Cohort Differences from 1989 to 2016." *Psychological Bulletin* (November 2017).
11. Fromm, Jeff and Read, Angie. *Marketing to Gen Z: The Rules for Reaching This Vast—and Very Different—Generation of Influencers* (New York: AMACOM, 2018): 29, 73.

INDEX

Pro method, for sending videos, 105–106, 108
Prospecting. *See* Cold prospecting

Q

QuickTime, 100

R

Read, Angela, 181
Recording videos:
    appearance and sound in, 118–121,
        143, 181
    approachability communicated in, 126
    authenticity and imperfections in,
        120–123, 133, 177, 181
    barriers to, 117–118
    calls to action in, 124, 154–155, 158
    camera angle for, 40, 77, 128–129, 133, 141
    comfort level with, improving, 116–131, 181
    connection developed in, 120–121, 157
    demographic considerations and, 180–181
    email tools for, 68, 105
    empathy expression in, 124, 125
    eye contact during, 129
    future of, 176, 179–181
    informality of, 12
    integrated access to, 106
    Internet connections for live, 141, 142
    iterative process of, 127–128
    length of, 9, 21, 74, 83, 91, 111–112, 153
    lighting for, 130, 133, 134, 137, 141, 144
    looking into lens during, 129
    marketing using professional, 11, 12, 22,
        62, 133, 136, 171
    mobile phones for, 62, 99–100, 102–104,
        129, 133, 135–136, 138, 139,
        141–143, 180
    outlines for, 122–123, 129
    overcoming barriers to, 130–131
    personal and natural setting for, 155–157
    practice with, 128
    prerecorded videos (*see* Prerecorded
        evergreen videos)
    process for, 126–128, 158
    pro method of, 105–106, 108
    relationship building through (*see*
        Relationship building)

screen recording, 107–108
smiling while, 130
social media tools for, 12, 111–112
starting points for, 126–127
talking to one person during, 129, 157
time spent, 6, 9
tips for successful, 77, 128–130
trigger points for, 78–96, 127, 162
unscripted words for, 121–126, 129–130
value provided in, 124, 125, 176
video cameras and equipment for, 40, 77,
    128–129, 132–144, 176, 180
vulnerability in, 120–121, 177
web apps for, 106
webcams for, 100, 129, 133, 134,
    139, 141, 180
wider angle of, 40, 129, 141
Referrals, word of mouth, 52–54, 76
Regulatory compliance, 95–96, 109
Rehumanization:
    current and future status of, 175–185
    dehumanization vs., 29
    improving, 145–185
    personal videos for (*see* Personal videos)
    reasons and motivations for, 1–56
    recording and sending techniques and
        equipment for, 97–144
    timing and opportunities for, 57–96
Relationship building:
    checking in for maintaining, 89
    connection development and, 120–121,
        157, 177–179, 181
    future effective and satisfying,
        176–179, 181
    gratitude and appreciation for, 68
    health effects of, 178
    importance of, 32–34
    marketing through video vs., 11,
        12, 133, 136
    personal videos for, 11–13, 34, 61, 67,
        73–74, 76, 77, 89, 120–121, 133,
        157, 176–179, 181
    psychological proximity and, 5, 9, 13, 177
    soft edge focus on, 178–179
Reply rate:
    follow-ups to low, 169–170
    increasing, 155–158
    sales vs. support, 68–70, 76

T

Targeted messaging, 149, 151, 161
Teachers, video benefits for, 47, 59–61
Telephone calls. *See also* Mobile phones
    cold calling, 158–161
    as email alternative, 26
    fraudulent or spam, 26
    personal videos paired with, 74,
        93, 158, 167
    personal videos vs., 5
    relationship building with, 33
    robocalls, 26
Telephone Consumer Protection Act of
        1991 (US), 109
Telford, Lynne, 67
Text messaging:
    delivery of videos in, 112
    as email alternative, 26
    recording videos in, 12
    sending videos with, 108–109, 112
    tracking videos in, 109
Thank yous:
    internal communication of, 91
    personal video benefits for, 63, 64, 66–68,
        76, 92, 94–95
    prerecorded evergreen videos for,
        71, 79, 110
    as trigger points for video use, 94–95
Thorne, Michael, 62–64
Thumbnail images:
    personalized message in, 9, 49, 105, 153
    sending videos with, 101, 103–105,
        109, 110
    video plays increased with
        strong, 153–154
Time:
    of day, best for sending videos,
        69, 151
    email overcrafting taking excessive, 28
    to follow-ups, 164, 165, 167
    latent demand at later, 172–173
    length of videos, 9, 21, 74, 83, 91,
        111–112, 153
    reading email at convenient, 26
    recording videos, 6, 9
    to resolution of customer needs, 71
    saving, with personal videos, 74–75

trigger points for video use,
        78–96, 127, 162
    video conferencing at scheduled, 26
    viewing videos at convenient, 5–6,
        27, 55, 82
Tools, digital, disintermediation by, 51–52
Tracking analytics:
    bad news receipt confirmed by, 87
    follow-ups based on, 164, 173, 174
    future of, 176, 182–183
    outcome improvements using, 149–150
    sending videos methods with/without,
        103–105, 109, 110
    survey results on, 16
    time of viewing confirmed with, 26, 82
    viewing method effects on, 115
Trainers, video benefits for, 47
Transcription apps, 167
Treece, Becky, 67
Trigger points for video use:
    bad news or apologies as, 86–89
    checking in as, 89
    cold prospecting and first introductions as,
        79–80, 162
    emotional expression as, 96
    exceptions to, 78, 95–96
    "great to meet you" messages as,
        81–82
    holidays and special occasions as, 84–85
    internal communication as, 90–92
    invitations as, 92–93
    nurturing leads as, 80–81
    overview of, 78, 127
    project or process updates as, 82–84
    thank you as, 94–95
Trolling, 29
Twitter, 26, 112

U

Underperformance factors:
    clarity lack as, 148–149
    differentiation lack as, 150
    sincerity lack as, 148
    targeting lack as, 149
    tracking absence as, 149–150
Updates, project. *See* Project or
        process updates